OZ CLARKE

GW00367546

101 BEST WHITE & ROSÉ WINES

WINE BUYING GUIDE 2008

PAVILION

First published in 2008 by Pavilion Books
An imprint of
Anova Books Company Ltd
10 Southcombe Street
London W14 0RA

www.anovabooks.com
www.ozclarke.com

Editor Fiona Holman
Design Georgina Hewitt

A CIP catalogue for this book is available from the British Library

ISBN-13: 978-1-862-05787-6
ISBN-10: 1-862-05787-6

10 9 8 7 6 5 4 3 2 1

Printed and bound by G. Canale & C. spa, Italy

The information and prices in this book were correct to the best of our knowledge when we went to press. Although every care has been taken in the preparation of this book, neither the publisher nor the editors can accept any liability for any consequences arising from the use of information contained herein.

Acknowledgments
We would like to thank all the retailers, agents and individuals who have helped to source wine labels and bottle photographs.

Please bear in mind that wine is not made in infinite quantities – some of these may well sell out, but the following year's vintage should then become available. Prices are those which applied in autumn 2007. All prices listed are per 750ml bottle inclusive of VAT, unless otherwise stated. Remember that some retailers only sell by the case – which may be mixed.

Contents

Introduction

This wine guide is for the optimists among you. Those of you who feel the sap rise in your veins with the first rays of springtime sunshine, the first chance to sit out in the park at lunchtime or stop for a drink on the way home in the gentle evening sun. To me, springtime is the most wonderful season, not only because the whole world wakes up again after the dark dog days of winter, but because I always believe I have an endless smiling summer of cloudless skies, emerald meadows and golden beaches spreading for months ahead until autumn arrives and is almost welcome, so exhausted am I by the brilliance of summer.

The optimist never learns. But spring and summer must be about optimism, good weather and good times, and good wine to lift the spirits and quicken the pulse. So what I've done here is choose for the sole purpose of making spring and summer as enjoyable as possible. Much as I like light fresh reds, I decided to keep things simple by focussing on the wines that summer craves – bright, tangy whites, juicy pinks and foaming fizz. So that means you won't find big, oaky 14% alcoholic monsters here. Virtually every wine is less than 13.5% alcohol, and as many as possible are 12.5% or less. Nor will you find wildly expensive wallet-bashers. Some of the fizz is unavoidably above £10 – but all the dry whites and pinks are less than a tenner. And you'll find three different categories – For a tenner or less, Around £5, and Cheap and Cheerful, so that you can match your budget to the best wine possible at the price. So now you just need to see what takes your fancy, check your nearest supplier and start planning your picnic or barbecue in the sure knowledge that this year it will not rain.

For a white wine to work in summertime you have to be able to gulp it. There are many wonderful whites that are simply too rich, too oaky, too complex and complicated – and too expensive to merit anything other than contemplative, respectful sipping. Well, I may like them, but they aren't the wines for this guide. Snappy, refreshing whites are the wines for this guide. Tangy whites bristling with leafy acidity. Whites where their lushness is the ripeness of fruit, not the blast of alcohol and oak. And sometimes whites that are pale and ethereal, tasting of stones and apple peel, that might seem thin and dull in the depths of winter, but which are simple, undemanding heaven when the weather is right.

At last rosé is coming out of the shadows – not peeping nervously out, ready to duck back at the slightest sign of criticism, but proudly, self-confidently, rosy-cheeked and cherry-lipped, a sparkle in the eyes and a gurgle of pleasure in the throat. And it's about time because pink wine is a smashing drink. You only have to look at that lovely luminescent colour to feel perked up, and one good glug of soft, dry strawberry-scented Garnacha or Merlot will turn a meeting into a party in no time flat. The experts reckon we will be drinking 50% more dry rosés (as against the sweet California 'white' Zinfandel types) by 2010, and I'm delighted.

The days of sparkling wine meaning 'Champagne' – and only Champagne – if you wanted a wine that tasted half decent – are long gone. Australia, South Africa, California and New Zealand are all producing Champagne lookalikes at affordable prices. France itself, with Crémant de Bourgogne using the same grapes and production methods, is making even more keenly priced lookalikes, while England is starting to produce joyous fizz that even rivals the top end of Champagne. But that's not all. Italian Prosecco which was virtually confined to drinking by the tiny icy glass on holidays in Venice, is now all over the high street, with its soft fluffy fruit and foaming mousse. And Cava has thrown off its rustic, earthy image for something much fresher and finer – and yet you can still buy it for a fiver.

Wine finder

Index by country

Shiraz-Cabernet Rosé, Los Nucos, Luis Felipe Edwards, Valle Central 48

Shiraz Rosé Riserva, Casillero del Diablo, Concha y Toro, Central Valley 45

ENGLAND
Rosé
Chapel Down English Rosé 42
Sparkling
Bloomsbury Cuvée Merret, Ridgeview, West Sussex 58
English Sparkling Rosé, Chapel Down 61

FRANCE
VdP = Vin de Pays

White
Bergerac Sec, Sauvignon Blanc-Semillon, Domaine des Eyssards, South-West France 29
Bordeaux, Châteaux's Selection (Benoit Calvet), Sauvignon-Semillon, Bordeaux 39
Bourgogne Chardonnay, Domaine du Pavillon, Burgundy 14
Chablis, Burgundy
  Domaine Billaud-Simon 16
  Domaine Servin 19
Chardonnay, VdP d'Oc, Advocate, Domaine Saint Hilaire, Languedoc-Roussillon 24
Château Bonnet, Les Vignobles

André Lurton, Entre-Deux-Mers, Bordeaux 30
Cheverny, Delaille 27
Coteaux du Languedoc, Picpoul de Pinet, Domaine de Félines, Languedoc-Roussillon 30
Cuvée Pecheur, VdP du Comté Tolosan, South-West France 38
Cuvée de Richard, VdP du Comté Tolosan, South-West France 39
Gros-Manseng-Sauvignon, VdP des Côtes de Gascogne, Alain Brumont, South-West France 23
Mâcon-Uchizy, Raphaël Sallet/Dom. de l'Arfentière, Burgundy 19
VdP du Gers (Marks & Spencer), South-West France 39
Viognier, La Baume, Languedoc-Roussillon 35
Rosé
Costières de Nîmes, Rhône Valley
  Château Roubaud 43
  Château Guiot 44
Côtes de Provence, Château Saint Baillon, Provence 43
Le Froglet Rosé, VdP d'Oc, Languedoc-Roussillon 46
Sparkling
Cabernet Rosé Brut, Ackerman, Loire Valley 62
Champagne
  Blanc de Blancs (Waitrose) 57
  Deutz 56
  Fleury 56
  Charles Heidsieck 56

Oudinot 57, 61
Premier Cru (Union Champagne/Tesco) 59
Crémant de Bourgogne, Blason de Bourgogne, Caves de Bailly, Burgundy 62

GREECE
White
Hatzidakis, Santorini 17

HUNGARY
White
Pinot Grigio (Hilltop Neszmély/Marks & Spencer) 36
Riesling, Budai, Nyakas 32

ITALY
White
Fiano-Greco, A Mano, Puglia 27
Verdicchio dei Castelli di Jesi Classico, Moncaro 37
Rosé
Oyster Bay Rosé, Delegats, Hawkes Bay 44
Sparkling
Prosecco, Vigna Del Cuc, Case Bianche, Martino Zanetti, Veneto 59

NEW ZEALAND
White
Chardonnay, Explorers Vineyard 30
Chardonnay, Stoneleigh, Marlborough 20

TOP
101

BEST WHITE WINES

The world of dry white wines could be sliced down the middle – oaked on one side and unoaked on the other. That would imply vanilla-ish, creamy, weighty on the oaked side, and anything sharp, minerally or ethereal on the other. Well, thank goodness the white wine world is a bit more exciting than that nowadays. Even the oak-monster New World Chardonnays that we lapped up only a few years ago have toned themselves down – and if they haven't you won't find them in this guide as it's springtime and summer wines I'm trying to celebrate here. We do have oaked wines in the guide – so long as the oak influence is delicately done, and so long as the alcohol is reasonable.

When it comes to unoaked styles, I've gone for freshness, brightness, appetizing fruit and acidity at alcohol levels that are never above 13.5% and are more often at 12.5% or below. And in this exciting fistful of wines you will find Sauvignon Blancs from numerous places around the globe, you'll find Riesling, Semillon/Sauvignon blends and unoaked Chardonnays; but you will also find Albariños, Semillons, Pinot Gris, Viogniers, Grüner Veltliners from Austria, bone dry Santorini white from Greece, and many more, all chosen to make your place this summer the better place to be.

• The wines are listed in descending price order.

WHITES FOR A TENNER OR LESS

2005 Bourgogne Chardonnay, Domaine du Pavillon, Burgundy, France, 13% ABV
Oddbins, £9.99

'Bourgogne' on the label can cover a multitude of sins and can simply be a dustbin for any old vats that didn't work out. But this one comes from a single vineyard on the outskirts of Meursault village, some of whose vines are in the Meursault appellation. So you get a very attractive 'almost Meursault' for less than half price. It lacks the lush texture of the grand Meursaults but it does have a true flavour of oatmeal, dry peach and nut flesh with a touch of waxy texture that will deepen no end with a few years' age.

2007 Sauvignon Blanc, Floresta, Viña Santa Rita, Leyda Valley, Chile, 14% ABV
Berkmann, Waitrose, £9.99

New Zealand may still be the leader in the world Sauvignon Blanc stakes, but Chile is making a determined run on the rails. You need cool conditions to produce good Sauvignon Blanc, and Chile is planting more and more coastal land where the air is chilled right down by the icy Humboldt Current that flows up South America's coast from the Antarctic. These foggy, windy areas are redefining the thrilling, crunchy greenness that makes Sauvignon such a refreshing drink. The Leyda Valley is about as close as you can get to the coast and this wine tingles on your tongue. It smells of tomato leaf, blackcurrant leaf and gooseberries and the flavour is a torrent of lime, green apple, nettle and gooseberry all washing over a pebbly riverbed. Big, powerful, sharp, green and spanking fresh.

2005 Sauvignon Blanc-Semillon, Sandalford, Margaret River, Western Australia, 12.5% ABV **Oz Wines, £9.99**

Sauvignon-Semillon is the famous Bordeaux white blend of grapes, but you could just as well say it's the famous Margaret River blend because they do it equally effectively in the far west of Australia. This is bone dry but full textured, less aggressive than a New Zealand or South African Sauvignon, with an appetizing smell of coffee bean and blackcurrant leaf and a mellow nutty flavour tinged with leather to soften the zesty, citrus snap.

2001 Semillon, Mount Pleasant Elizabeth, McWilliam's, Hunter Valley, New South Wales, Australia, 11% ABV **Morrisons, £9.99**

This is not the kind of wine you expect to come across as you amble up the aisles of a supermarket which until recently largely prided itself on how many bottles it stocked at £2.99. This is a great old-fashioned Aussie classic from the Hunter Valley near Sydney. It's low in alcohol and has a brilliant, unique flavour of custard and nectarines, brioche and peach, orange peel and leather washed with beeswax that lingers in your mouth long after you've swallowed.

2006 Semillon, Steenberg, Constantia, South Africa, 14% ABV **Waitrose, £9.99**

Wow, those guys at Steenberg are good. Other trendy Cape wineries rise and fall but Steenberg stokes its fire every single vintage. They were one of the first to show how brilliantly South Africa could do cool climate whites. Loads of people do that now but no-one does it better than Steenberg. They are most famous for their tangy, leafy Sauvignon, but this Semillon is another star – fermented in oak barrels to impart a lush glycerol sheen to the wine and just a little vanilla spice, but that merely serves to accentuate the flood of apple and pear flesh juiciness and the stern stony dryness of the wine is tempered and soothed in the glass.

2006 Chablis, Domaine Billaud-Simon, Burgundy, France, 12% ABV
H & H Bancroft, The Wine Society and other independent retailers, £9.95

The label states, 'Our purpose: to offer an ethereal, crystalline Chablis emotion…' What a delightful idea. And how well they've achieved it. Too many modern Chablis are tasting positively creamy in an unwelcome move towards disowning their birthright. I like ripe Chablis, sure, but this is as ripe as it needs to be and it's only 12 per cent alcohol. Push this up to 13.5 by minimizing the yield and leaving what grapes are left to overripen into the autumn, and you lose the whole point of Chablis.

As it is, this is very pure, ripe but delicate, intense yet ethereal. Cool white apple flesh and mellow lemon acidity softened just a little by brioche yeast then brought back into line with a finely judged – yes, 'crystalline' – minerality. Beautifully balanced classic Chablis.

2006 Chardonnay, McLean's Farm, Barossa Valley, South Australia, 13% ABV
Oz Wines, £8.99

Bob McLean is a big, beefy fellow, generous and jovial, and I thought his Chardonnay would reflect this big, bluff style. But Bob is also a keen observer of the tides that sweep wine styles back and forth, and he knows that we like our Chardonnays a little more subtle nowadays. So, despite the fruit coming from Kalimna – a vineyard famous for providing brawny, succulent Shiraz grapes to one of Australia's greatest red wines, Penfolds Grange – this is gentle, scented with peach blossom, flavoured with apple and melon flesh. I'd almost say it was feminine, but Bob knows where I live. He'd never let me get away with it.

2006 Grüner Veltliner, Obere Steigen, Huber, Traisental, Austria,
12.5% ABV **Oddbins, £8.99**

Many Grüner Veltliners are marked out by a strong and appetizing flavour of white
pepper. This one is a little riper and softer than usual, and has a different way of
expressing its freshess – a spritzy prickle on the palate, a scent of sandalwood
that is bone dry, and full white flesh that has a little grapefruit pith sharpness
but is mostly juicy and fat.

2006 Hatzidakis, Santorini, Greece, 13.5% ABV
Halifax Wine Company, £8.99

Santorini is one of the Mediterranean's great experiences: the remains of a vast
volcanic eruption has left a heart-stopping crescent bay, mighty cliffs and dark
grey volcanic ash now turned to soil. Such extreme surroundings should produce
exceptional wines – and they do. Assyrtiko is the local grape, and its wines always
have an unnerving rock dust rasp to them, a real mineral growl, but this is evened
out by excellent ripe green apple and ripe lemon flavours, and a savoury scent
halfway between pepper and lovage.

2006 Riesling, Polish Hill River, O'Leary Walker, Clare Valley, South
Australia, 12.5% ABV **Waitrose, £8.99**

My mum's name is O'Leary, so I was always going to like this one. It shows the
fascinating paradox of Clare Valley Riesling – able to be aggressive and snappy
yet reassuringly full (*not* a description of my mum). Strong, stony green apple fruit
is given extra gooseberry and lemon zest snap and then fattened up with the flesh
of a baked apricot.

2004 Riesling, Show Reserve, Arrowfield Estate, Great Southern, Western Australia,
12.5% ABV **Oddbins, £8.99**

A Riesling from the broad empty acres of Western Australia's bottom end. The potential for quality is tremendous down here: the trouble is there is hardly any water available – and, of course, with no people, no passing trade to help the cashflow. Even so, what wine they do manage to squeeze out of their cool but arid earth is delicious. This is lovely Riesling – quite rich in texture, but this glycerine softness is easily overwhelmed by a citrus slap of lime zest, the rasp of vineyard stones and the passing whiff of petrol spilt from the pump.

2007 Viognier-Pinot Gris, Heartland,
Langhorne Creek-Limestone Coast,
South Australia, 13.5% ABV
**deFINE, Great Western Wine, Oddbins,
Playford Ros, Selfridges, Tanners, Noel
Young and other independent retailers,
£8.95–£9.99**

All the lushness of Australian fruit with none of the sullen oak. This is delectable and inspiringly original in flavour – scented pear and apricot flesh, pithy lemon acidity and uplifting lime flower aroma to titillate your nostrils.

2006 Mâcon-Uchizy, Raphaël Sallet/Domaine
de l'Arfentière, Burgundy, France, 13% ABV
Roger Harris Wines, £8.50

Uchizy is one of the best villages in the Mâconnais, but
one of the least known – probably because it sounds
like an invalid sneezing. Consequently you can get real
Burgundy class for a fair price. This is delightful wine,
not overblown, keenly balanced, a mix of ripe apple
and slightly unripe peach before it's really softened,
a soothing texture of savoury cream and a splash
of honey.

2006 Chablis, Domaine Servin, Burgundy, France, 12.5% ABV
Majestic, £8.49

Ah, what a delight. The calm, cool voice of reason – a lightly chilled, bone dry, well-mannered wine. It's soft,
but only in terms of not sporting rough edges or rawness, it has lovely fluffy apple fruit, the acidity of ripe
lemon peel and a cool undertow of pebbles. Mmm.

2005 Chardonnay, Stoneleigh, Marlborough, New Zealand, 14.5% ABV
Threshers, £8.49 (3 for 2, £5.66)

This is a great Chardonnay bargain when you buy it as 3 for 2. New Zealand makes some of the world's best Chardonnays, often in quite small volumes, but this is made in decent quantities, to a very high standard, by a division of the global giant Pernod Ricard. It combines intense fruit with really 'Burgundian' oak flavours. What does this mean? OK: the fruit is bright and fresh, melons and eating apples, juicy but pale. The oak aging has added an almost syrupy richness of oatmeal, brazil nuts, toasted cashews and a texture of beeswax. And that's special.

2006 Albariño, Rías Baíxas, Val do Sosego (Bodegas As Laxas), Galicia, Spain, 12.5% ABV **Oddbins, £7.99**

White from Spain's cool, wet north-west, where the Atlantic storms dump more rain than in Manchester. Thankfully it's also hotter than Manchester, so grapes can ripen, up to a point. But they never lose the sense of cool and moisture. This wine is soft, even slightly chubby, but that only serves as a vehicle for the cool fruit of pears and white peach and the pithy bitterness of grapefruit zest. And all the time you sense the grass glistening with dew, the cliff rocks washed with rain.

2006 Chardonnay, Twin Wells, Hunter Valley, New South Wales, Australia, 13% ABV **Marks & Spencer, £7.99**

Hunter Valley Chardonnays from north of Sydney were the first Aussie Chardonnays to become famous in Britain, but that was a long time ago and we'd find them pretty yellow and oily nowadays. Modern Hunter Chardonnays are still on the fat side, but far better balanced. This is a good example, with a leather and beeswax texture, gentle apple and nut fruit flavour and a warm-climate aroma of smoke tinged with a wisp of petrol fumes.

2007 Riesling, Tim Adams, Clare Valley, South Australia, 12% ABV
Tesco, £7.99

If you want to experience the pure, crystalline nature of Australian Riesling, Tim Adams does it as well as any. His wine is full, but dry and austere, minerally dry flecked with lemon sherbet, green apple core and lime zest. Chill it down. Love it.

2005 Riesling, Magnus, Leasingham Wines, Clare Valley, South Australia, 12.5% ABV
Sainsbury's, Somerfield, Threshers, Noel Young, £7.99–£8.99

Leasingham is a big operation and they make big-boned Rieslings, which is a bit paradoxical: weight, power and citrus delicacy. You find quite a lot of paradoxes – between light and weighty, green-scented and jam-rich – in Australia's Clare Valley, in both reds and whites. This still has loads of lemon and orange peel zip, apple and melon fruit, but also a little leathery fatness and petrol tank aroma.

2007 Sauvignon Blanc, Dashwood, Marlborough, New Zealand, 13.5% ABV
Oddbins, £7.99

One of the most consistently high quality yet affordable Kiwi Sauvignons on the market. I use it in tastings all around the country and it never lets me down. It pings with mouthwatering green-fleshed fruit – apples and lime, nettles and gooseberry and even an exotic drop of passionfruit. Ripe and tangy. Very good.

2006 Sauvignon Blanc, M'Hudi, Elgin, South Africa, 13% ABV
Marks & Spencer, £7.99

I met the guys who make this wine last year. It's a Black Empowerment project. Sometimes you think the political purpose outweighs the wine quality, but sometimes you just know this one will work. M'hudi's like that. The guys are top guys, using top grapes from the cool highlands of Elgin. And the wine has that smashing, fizzing, ultra-green quality of good Cape Sauvignon. It's very dry, but attractively soft, yet the flavour is a rip-tide of nettles and coffee beans, lime leaf and juicy green apple.

2006 Sauvignon Blanc, Limited Selection, Montes, Leyda Valley, Chile, 13.5% ABV
Majestic, £7.99

Montes makes several Sauvignons, but this is my favourite – from the foggy coastal vineyards of Leyda, an area which is proving to be a star performer, particularly for Sauvignon and Pinot Noir. This is all green and fresh and outdoors. Nectarine and greengage, green apple, lime zest and nettles all crunch together with a mineral coolness.

2006 Sauvignon Blanc, Classic Reserve, Viña Leyda, Leyda Valley, Chile, 13.5% ABV
Playford Ros, £7.49

This is marvellous tangy stuff, a great riot of green sharp flavours, yet the end sensation is ripe, not raw. Grapefruit and gooseberry, passionfruit and blackcurrant leaf, lime zest and nettles all foaming over your tongue like a wave breaking along the beach.

2005 Gros Manseng-Sauvignon, Vin de Pays des Côtes de Gascogne, Alain Brumont, South-West France, 12.5% ABV
Green & Blue, £7.45

Alain Brumont is a great red wine producer in France's South-West, but he's decided on a very interesting white combination here – the sharp Gros Manseng and the aromatic Sauvignon – and it works. It's a lovely, full, challenging mix of tropical and green, nectarine and peach and pear in an off-dry relationship with lemon zest and leaves plucked from a pepper tree.

DOMAINE
SAINT HILAIRE

ADVOCATE
CHARDONNAY 2005
VIN DE PAYS D'OC

2005 Chardonnay, Vin de Pays d'Oc, Advocate, Domaine Saint Hilaire, Languedoc-Roussillon, France, 13.5% ABV
Christopher Piper Wines, £7.26

Spot-on Chardonnay for those of you who don't like the thick-headed stodgy style so many New World Chardonnays have adopted. This wine is from an excellent single estate in southern France. It does have some oak influence, but very subtly applied, in the French manner: melon and apple fruit – fresh, not squashy – a little apple peel rasp to sharpen the palate, and a mild, spicy, nutty oak veneer that makes no attempt to dominate the wine.

2006 Riesling, Daniel Schuster, Waipara, New Zealand, 10.5% ABV
les Caves de Pyrene, £7.04

Given that Australia makes many superb Rieslings in relatively warm conditions, the cool-loving Riesling really should be seen more in New Zealand. Maybe its relative scarcity is simply because we won't buy it. Well, Waipara is well down the South Island towards Christchurch – brilliant cool conditions – and this delicate, fragrant example is a delight: only 10.5% alcohol and an absurdly drinkable mélange of orange, lime and peach, scratched with the mineral lick of stones and not quite dry.

2005 Chardonnay, Yering Frog, Yering Station, Yarra Valley, Victoria, Australia, 14% ABV
Majestic, £6.99

Balance is what marks the delicate but tasty Chardonnays of the Yarra Valley near Melbourne. Gentle, spicy oak marries effortlessly with a soft, almost dilute, acidity, mellow apple fruit and a warm cream and nut syrup softness. Everything in balance. The Yarra Valley is a very expensive area, yet this is a quid or two less than the rubbish South East Australian Chardonnays that bestrew the high street. Of course, this holds its price. No one in their right mind buys the rubbish brands until they're slashed to £3.99.

2007 Sauvignon Blanc, Secano Estate, Leyda Valley, Chile, 13.5% ABV
Marks & Spencer, £6.99

I'm delighted to see the wines of Leyda spreading rapidly into the high street and the supermarkets. This brand new coastal area of Chile hit the ground running with some of the most spanking fresh Sauvignons the world had seen only a couple of years ago. As the vines have got older, the wines have become fuller, but lost none of their brilliantly, aromatically aggressive turmoil of capsicum, gooseberry, celery, nettle and lime zest. Exhilarating stuff.

2007 Sauvignon Blanc, Ormonde Cellars, Darling, South Africa, 12% ABV
Tesco, £6.99

All up the west coast of South Africa we're discovering more and more excellent cool-climate sites that particularly shine with Sauvignon. The flavours are different to those of New Zealand: they're leaner, more aggressive, less full of tropical fruit and lime zest. This is a good example, from the Darling Hills – tangy but full-bodied, with the sharpness of nettles, the juiciness of green apples and the drying flavours of summer earth and freshly roasted coffee beans.

2006 Sauvignon Blanc, Explorers Vineyard, New Zealand, 13% ABV
Co-op, £6.99

The Explorers label is always worth seeking out at the Co-op; like the Dashwood (see page 22), this is one of the best-priced Kiwi Sauvignons in the country. It's got good stabbing gooseberry, lime zest and nettles and a streak of metallic mineral. Full bodied, but aggressively zesty with it.

2006 Chardonnay Reserva, Viña Porta, Bío Bío Valley, Chile, 13.5% ABV
Threshers, £6.49 (3 for 2, £4.33)

An intelligent mix of Chardonnay grapes from Bío Bío in the cool damp south and Chile's much warmer Central Valley. There's no splodge of oak to detract from the flavours, so you get a very easy, pleasant, fresh style dominated by pear, apple and melon flesh tarted up with a flicker of spicy cream.

2006 Cheverny, Le Vieux Clos, Delaille, Loire Valley, France, 12.5% ABV
Majestic, £6.49

What a delightful surprise. This is 85% Sauvignon and 15% Chardonnay from what can only be described as one of the lesser byways of the Loire Valley. But it's delicious. It's aggressive, but that's exactly what most boring modern Loire whites lack. This is a riot of pith and leaf (pronounce that after a couple) – blackcurrant leaf, grapefruit and lemon pith, white melon flesh, coffee bean scent – all just softened a little by the 15% Chardonnay. I recall not too long ago when Sancerre used to make wines like this. Until she remembers how to again, I shall have to drink Cheverny.

2006 Fiano-Greco, A Mano, Puglia, Italy, 12.5% ABV
Booths, Hedley Wright, Philglas & Swiggot, Villeneuve, Noel Young and other independent retailers, £6.49–£6.99

Delightful coupling of two of southern Italy's most interesting grape varieties from the unlikely arid area of the heel of Italy – Puglia. You'd expect Puglian whites to be bleached and baked by the sun, but this one is spritzy fresh, with loads of fruit flavour, a touch of floral scent, a gentle acidity like boiled lemons – zest and all – backed up by pastry softness.

2006 The Best Chilean Sauvignon Blanc, Curicó Valley, Chile, 13% ABV
Morrisons, £6.49

The label says this Sauvignon is from the warm Curicó Valley, but I'll wager good money there's more than a splash of high-quality cool-climate fruit in the blend, because the ripeness is matched with streaks and shards of grapefruit pith, green apple and lemon zest.

2006 Chardonnay, Block 66, Kingston Estate, Padthaway, South Australia, 13.5% ABV
Averys, £6.29

Here's a producer who understands quality, personality and a sensible price. I associate Kingston Estate with full-blooded reds, not Chardonnay. Never mind. Down in the fairly upmarket region of Padthaway, famous for very serious Chardonnays, they've come up with a very attractive spicy modern Chardie with just a hint of that traditional leather and fat fruit Aussie thing. It's fresh, it's bright and it has an aftertaste of peach blossom scent in spring.

WHITES FOR AROUND £5

2006 Albariño, Rías Baíxas, Galicia, Spain, 12.5% ABV
Sainsbury's Taste the difference, £5.99

This is a little chubbier than I expected, but that isn't too much of a problem, because the traditional Galician austerity soon muscles past the puppy fat, the stewed, barely ripe apple fruit turns towards mint perfume and stones and the final effect is of the rocky coastline, the wild Atlantic weather and a flavour washed endlessly by fresh summer rain.

2005 Bergerac Sec, Sauvignon Blanc-Sémillon, Domaine des Eyssards, South-West France, 13% ABV
Waitrose, £5.99

Bergerac's vineyards are basically the same as Bordeaux's; it's purely an administrative boundary between the *départements* of Gironde and Dordogne that demands a change of name. The grapes they grow are the same and this Sauvignon-Sémillon – the classic white Bordeaux blend – has good waxy weight from the Sémillon and a spring shower of sharp green flavours and scents: capsicum, nettle, blackcurrant leaf and grapefruit as well as the juicy fruit of ripe apple and pear. There's even a touch of spritz to tingle your tongue.

2006 Château Bonnet, Les Vignobles André Lurton, Entre-Deux-Mers, Bordeaux, France, 12% ABV Sainsbury's, £5.99

Are we ever going to give Bordeaux whites the acclaim they deserve? Our disdain for their charms keeps the price low, and we really should take advantage, because I can't believe the fickle finger of fashion won't point back in their direction some time soon. André Lurton is one of Bordeaux's great white winemakers and Bonnet is his home. This is some home brew – wonderfully textured , a little fatter than you might expect (he puts 10% Muscadelle in the blend), but it's a sort of pear flesh and banana fatness, and this is thrillingly balanced by grapefruit and lemon zest and the crunchy, chewy bitter sweetness of apple core.

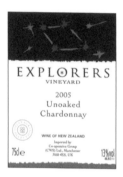

2005 Unoaked Chardonnay, Explorers Vineyard, New Zealand, 13% ABV Co-op, £5.99

Oak can be used to hide the deficiencies in Chardonnay fruit: the vanilla and spice of barrels provides great make-up. So if you're going to make a successful *unoaked* Chardonnay, the fruit must be of good quality. In which case New Zealand is a good place to go, since she grows some of the world's best Chardonnay. This one has delightful greengage and apple fruit, fattened up with some nuts, and honeyed from having its creamy yeast lees stirred up with the wine in the tank, and there's a slight suggestion of white pepper.

2005 Coteaux du Languedoc, Picpoul de Pinet, Domaine de Félines, Languedoc-Roussillon, France, 13% ABV Waitrose, £5.99

I never quite know how Picpoul de Pinet manages to make such fresh wine in such a torrid part of France's Mediterranean coast, but it's been famous for generations as the far south's smartest white. Well, the grape's name gives you a clue: Picpoul means 'lipstinger' in old French, and it's one of the few white grapes that could keep its acidity in such super-hot conditions. Most Picpoul is made by the co-op and is fair, but single estates are much better. This has a very nice apple and pear flavour, maybe the apple is just a little bruised, and there's a pleasant hint of almond. And the acidity? It's there.

2006 Pinot Gris, Finca Las Higueras, Lurton, Mendoza, Argentina, 13% ABV
Waitrose, £5.99

The Lurtons are whizz-kid entrepreneurs and winemakers from Bordeaux in France, but they make extremely good wine all over the world. They've planted a vineyard in Argentina, high up towards the Andes, where they make Pinot Gris with real flavour – unlike a lot of the hyper-dilute examples we're being offered from Italy under the disturbingly trendy Pinot Grigio tag. This would do just as well for a light lunch white, but it has taste – full, ripe, redolent of pears, flavoured with apple, coated in cream.

2007 Chardonnay-Verdelho-Semillon, Stickleback White, Heartland Wines, South Australia, 12.5% ABV
The Wine Society, £5.95

The description 'fresh, crisp, zesty' is not one I would normally apply to Australian Chardonnay. But this is made by the cutting edge Heartland operation, and when they promise you something, they deliver. What the winemaker has done here is to mix the plump Chardonnay with the acid Verdelho and the lean Semillon, pick all the grapes early so that the alcohol level is only 12.5%, and not let his precious liquid anywhere near an oak barrel. And it works. Green apple crunchiness is the most obvious flavour, fleshed out with a glyceriney fullness and a waft of smoky yeast softness. Fresh, crisp, zesty? Pretty much.

2006 Riesling, Budai, Nyakas, Hungary, 12.5% ABV
Wines of Westhorpe, £5.70

Hungary isn't known for its Riesling, but it does have many cool vineyard areas where Riesling might thrive. I could mistake this for an Australian Riesling – that's a compliment – because it's bone dry, with a concentrated green apple peel, greengage and grapefruit core, sharp lemon peel acidity and the rough rub of stones.

2005 The Society's Chilean Chardonnay (Viña Concha y Toro), Casablanca Valley, Chile, 13.5% ABV
The Wine Society, £5.50

The Wine Society used to favour Chardonnays which were good, but erred slightly on the tweed and old school tie side of things. This is much more modern, positively scented and, dare I say it, ever so slightly feminine – mixing melon and honey and mineral dryness with a scent that's like a floral and nut-based face cream. Now, which is it? Is it L'Oreal, or Caudalie, or Dior …?

2006 La Basca Uvas Blancas, Vino de la Tierra de Castilla y León, Spain, 13% ABV Marks & Spencer, £5.49

Telmo Rodríguez is one of Spain's hottest young winemakers, and it's fantastic to see M&S hitching up with guys of such talent. What he's done here is to take the Verdejo and Viura grapes – both very dry, veering on the neutral in style – and create a dry wine full of sharp fruit – green nettle and grapefruit – spanking fresh and smelling of bananas and pears, and to counter its weight in the mouth, roughed up by the dryness of riverbed pebbles.

2005 Riesling, Eaglehawk, Wolf Blass, South Eastern Australia, 11.5% ABV Sainsbury's, £5.49

Wolf Blass is a massive operation and most of its wines at this price level are entirely unmemorable. But this shows they *can* do the business if they want to. This is delightful dry Riesling, with good apple fruit, lashings of lemon zest and lemon juice acidity and a softness like leathery cream. It's a little mellower than some Aussie Rieslings but at £5.49 it might persuade an uncertain British public into trying Riesling wine. Riesling, by the way, is often the best of the Big Brands' offerings: Jacob's Creek is good too.

2006 Semillon, Peter Lehmann, Barossa Valley, South Australia, 11.5% ABV Tesco, £5.49

What a joy to see Peter Lehmann appearing more in our high streets once again: he is Australia's past master at giving value to his customers by dint of fair prices and fabulous flavours. And these flavours are untamed. If you're faint

of heart and fearsome of new experiences, leave this wine alone. But if you like the sound of a bone-dry wine that is almost rocky in its seriousness, and yet which combines the scent of fresh leather with the richness of orange custard, the crunchiness of apple flesh and the searing essential oil acidity of lemon zest to choke the unwary – this is a must.

2006 Ribatejo, Portal da Águia, Portugal, 12.5% ABV
Oddbins, £4.99

Portugal isn't just about reds – it does good, individual whites as well and, in the main, from grape varieties unheard of anywhere else. This time it's the Arinto and the Fernão Pires and they make a pretty good pair, with all the come-hither being provided by white peach, melon and pear flesh juiciness, and a slight note of adult caution provided by zesty grapefruit pith and a streak of minerality like a shining rapier blade.

2006 Rueda, Casa del Sol, Sauvignon Blanc-Verdejo, Agricola Castellana, Castilla y León, Spain, 13% ABV
Co-op, £4.99

The white wines of Rueda, from north-west Spain, have the great ability to seem quite fat and soft, yet to be suffused with green sharp flavours. Maybe it's the paradox of their origins – a parched high plain of gaunt pebbly earth, boiled by day, frozen by night. This example is quite full, with some soft cream and nut texture, but the character of the wine is green peel, green flesh and coffee bean flavour, tautened by bleached stones.

2006 Torrontés, Norton, Mendoza, Argentina, 12.5% ABV
Oddbins, £4.99

Most of Mendoza is too hot to make really fragrant Torrontés (you need the high mountain valleys) but I visited Norton's Torrontés vineyards with the guy who farms them and though they were within spitting distance of the heat-seeking Malbecs, he swore they made lovely wine. And they do. Classic, unashamed Torrontés: grape flesh richness sharpened by grapefruit, then wrapped in pastry, scythed apart by pungent lime zest and leaving a lingering aroma of lemon blossom.

2006 Viognier, Trivento, Mendoza, Argentina, 13.5% ABV
Waitrose, £4.99

This is made in Argentina by Chile's biggest wine producer, Concha y Toro. They've planted hundreds of acres in Argentina's best valleys, especially the cool Tupungato – and cool is of enormous importance in making good whites in the generally pretty torrid Argentine. This is delightful, fresh, bright, not at all complicated but exceedingly drinkable, with scented apricot fruit and a mouthwatering nip of acidity.

2006 Viognier, La Baume, Winemaker's Selection, Languedoc-Roussillon, France, 13.5% ABV
Waitrose, £4.99

This has such a lovely rich spicy quality I thought it had been aged in new oak barrels. But then I thought, not at a price tag of £4.99 – and so I checked. No oak. Pure fruit. This exotic heady spice comes from the grape, the same grapes that give fruit simply oozing with lush apricot juice, the same grapes that provide beguiling floral scent and resinous zesty grapefruit to keep everything fresh.

CHEAP AND CHEERFUL WHITES

2006 Hungarian Pinot Grigio (Hilltop Neszmély), 12.5% ABV
Marks & Spencer, £4.29

Hungarian Pinot Gris is fantastically good. Some traditions have it that the Pinot Gris grape variety comes from there, so we should pay these Danube delights a bit more respect. This isn't quite dry, and has an utterly charming flavour of white and pink apple flesh, honeydew melon and the restrained zesty acidity of boiled lemons.

2006 Sauvignon Blanc, Excelsior Estate, Robertson, South Africa, 12.5% ABV
Waitrose, £4.29

South Africa is making a lot of good Sauvignon Blanc nowadays and there are few better places to grow it than Robertson, with its limestone soils (which Sauvignon and Chardonnay love) and cool breezes winding up the Breede River Valley. Add to this the fact that the Excelsior Estate is biodynamically farmed and I'm not surprised at the green apple peel and nettle leaf freshness of this wine, though it's a little softer than many Cape Sauvignons.

2005 Chardonnay Reserve, Bushland
(Hope Estate), Hunter Valley, New South Wales,
Australia, 13% ABV
Aldi, £3.99

Aldi introduced this last year to rave reviews. This is the
new vintage and it's just as good. Real, serious, deep Chardonnay from one of Australia's most expensive
regions – and check the price! Maybe it's because this style of Chardonnay has gone out of fashion a bit.
Well, I can understand. It's not sleek and modern, but it's packed with fat peach fruit and nut syrup, it's got a
savoury leather scent and a smooth waxy texture. For £3.99? Take a punt.

2005 Verdicchio dei Castelli di Jesi Classico, Moncaro, Marche, Italy, 12.5% ABV
Waitrose, £3.99

Good, full, direct, tasty Italian white. It hasn't got all kinds of complex flavours – very few Italian whites
have – but you do get that fluffy soft flesh of a ripe apple and the sharp crunch of the peel, a hint of
lemon and a smear of honeyed cream.

2006 Pinot Grigio, Recas, Romania, 12.5% ABV
Wines of Westhorpe, £3.93

If only Pinot Grigios at £2 more had half as much character as this. Romania has been growing Pinot Grigio for ever and her wines are packed with personality – banana and pear, raw apple and a sharp squirt of lemon. It makes for an excellent white. I hope someone buys it.

2006 Cuvée Pecheur, Vin de Pays du Comté Tolosan, South-West France, 11.5% ABV
Waitrose, £3.49

The Gascony region of South-West France traditionally grew grapes to make Armagnac brandy. As demand for that fell away, they've started turning the acid, green grapes into splendidly refreshing, tart, sharp but fruity dry white wines. This is spitting with green leaf and apple peel venom. If you like this style – it's like a tangy Sauvignon in all but name – South-West France offers you the world's best value.

2006 Vin de Pays du Gers (white), South-West France, 11.5% ABV
Marks & Spencer, £3.49

Another nice snappy fresh dry white from South-West France. This is relatively soft, but that doesn't get in the way of lemon pith zing, green apple fruit and a hint of herbs and peppercorn. Tesco also has a version, at £2.99, called Vieille Fontaine Blanc.

2006 Bordeaux, Chateaux's Selection (Benoit Calvet), Sauvignon-Semillon, Bordeaux, France, 12% ABV
Aldi, £3.29

Good, citrous dry white wine at a very good price. Lemon and grapefruit zest blending cheerily with apple and melon fruit and a hint of nutty yeast to soften it.

2006 Cuvée de Richard (white), Vin de Pays du Comté Tolosan, South-West France, 11.5% ABV
Majestic, £3.19

All the good guys turn up in Gascony for their French house white. This is snappy, sharp, but not raw, with lots of grapefruit zest, apple peel and fresh citrus juice acidity.

BEST ROSÉ WINES

I'm not going to give you complicated, poetic tasting notes about the pink wines, because any half-decent rosé shouldn't have anything complicated to write about. It should sport a come-hither bright fresh colour, a fresh, inviting aroma and a happy party and picnic easygoing flavour, whether bone dry or not quite. These are good-time gluggers. And they're becoming very popular. Last year we noted a huge increase in their popularity. This year supermarkets report pink sales shooting ahead again, often up 50 per cent. So here are the pick of the pinks.

Rosé has been the traditional summer drink in the South of France and Spain for generations, but it hasn't always been very good. Provence rosé, in particular, has usually been thin and over-priced. Well, the rest of southern France has now started sending us cheaper and tastier pinks, and Spain is showing cracking form with its rosados. But it's the New World that has really taken up the pink baton and is running like fury with it. Chile's juicy, super-tasty examples are leading the way. Don't forget England, either, with its delicate, light examples.

- My favourite rosé this year also happens to be the most expensive and therefore the first in this section; after that I've listed wines in descending price order.

ROSÉS FOR A TENNER OR LESS

2005 Zweigelt, Langenloiser Rosé, Trocken, Bründlmayer, Kamptal, Austria, 12% ABV
Bacchus, Raeburn, Sommelier, £9.99

I'm tempted to say that this is a pink you must take seriously. It's from the excellent Zweigelt grape grown in excellent vineyards by one of Austria's greatest winemakers; he'd say, chill it down. Drink it. End of story. But I have to tell you, it's got a fabulous flavour of apple flesh and strawberry, radishes and a spray of white pepper.

2006 Chapel Down English Rosé, 11.5% ABV
Waitrose, £8.99

This is a mix of white grapes and red – especially new red varieties Rondo and Regent, which give great flavour and colour even under the pale English sun. Well, it isn't pale any more, of course, but our reds still need a bit of help ripening. However, red grapes that aren't quite ripe can make smashing rosé – and this has a lovely smoky apple flavour, a cream cheese texture tempered by summer earth and a gentle, ripe red fruit aftertaste.

2007 Côtes de Provence rosé, Château Saint Baillon, Provence, France, 12.5% ABV
Goedhuis & Co, £7.74

Côtes de Provence pinks are some of the most expensive in France, and with a captive audience dying of thirst on the local beaches every summer, willing to suck up any old stuff at a silly price, we don't see much Provence rosé over here. But this one's good – fleshy for Provence, but still dry, with mildly squashy apple fruit and a hint of rich date ripeness.

2005 Costières de Nîmes rosé, Cuvée Prestige, Château Roubaud, Rhône Valley, France, 13% ABV
Yapp Brothers, £7.60

The Rhône Valley makes a lot of really nice rosé. Some of the best comes from the far south, where the vineyards are stony and warm – and this wine is deep, stony, mouthfilling with glycerine texture and full of apple and strawberry fruit.

2006 Ribera del Duero rosado, El Quintanal, Castilla y León, Spain, 13% ABV
Oddbins, £7.49

Ribera del Duero makes some of the most serious, sought-after red wine in Spain. But that doesn't stop them wanting a drop of something more light-hearted – this is fresh, creamy and full flavoured, but chill it down and it does the trick.

2006 Muga Rosado, Rioja, Spain, 13.5% ABV
Waitrose, £6.99

Sophisticated stuff. Muga are known for making very serious, highly sought after Rioja reds. But even the most serious guys need to have a bit of fun – not too much fun, no dancing on the tables, just loosening the tie and cracking a smile. So this should do nicely. The grapes for this wine come from the two best vineyard areas in Rioja. The majority are Garnacha which gives a lovely spicy, heady plum fruit and cream texture. Most of the rest are white Viura that gives a lean, snappy acidity and a bright perfume of pears.

2007 Oyster Bay Rosé, Delegats, Hawkes Bay, New Zealand, 13% ABV
Sainsbury's, £6.99

The one thing that New Zealand always guarantees you is a wine with lots of flavour, even in its pinks. They simply don't know how to produce flavourless grapes, and even the Merlot which can produce pretty bland stuff, is full of life in Kiwi hands. The colour of the wine is quite marked here, but the flavour is more that of a crisp, ripe eating apple – gentle yet refreshing, a squirt of moreish acidity balancing a creamy mellowness in the mouth.

2006 Costières de Nîmes Rosé, Château Guiot, Rhône Valley, France, 13.5% ABV
Majestic, £6.24

This is a powerful, rumbustious pink – with loads of strawberry but also some windfall apples, syrup richness damped down with stony dry weight, and a welcome hint of herbs.

2006 Cabernet Sauvignon Rosé, San Medín, Miguel Torres, Curicó Valley, Chile, 13.5% ABV
Waitrose, £5.99

Great grape, great winemaker – and this wine's for drinking, not philosophizing. Even so, for a rosé, it's bulging, it's rippling with blackcurrant fruit and strawberry syrup. Rich but balanced and good. Very tasty.

2006 Marques de Rojas Rosado, Bodegas Piqueras, Almansa, Castilla-La Mancha, Spain, 13.5% ABV
Averys, £5.99

It gets pretty hot in Almansa, inland from Alicante, and I suspect the Syrah grape struggles a bit under the relentless sun. But it still produces a pretty tasty pink – creamy in style, full in texture, but with quite enough pear, apple and strawberry fruit to make it an enjoyable drink.

2006 Casillero del Diablo Shiraz Rosé, Viña Concha y Toro, Central Valley, Chile, 13.5% ABV
Waitrose, £5.99

I'm not used to seeing the title 'Reserva' on a bottle of rosé. This usually means the wine is quite dense and has been aged in oak. Well, not here it doesn't. Reserva simply means a bit more intense, a bit tastier. To be honest, Chilean rosés have so much flavour in any case, you don't want extra, but this is about right – deep, dry red fruit – dry being the operative word – cooled down and calmed by fresh acidity and a veil of rock dust twinkling through the wine.

2006 Slowine Rosé, South Africa, 13% ABV
Butlers, Flagship, Christopher Piper Wines, £5.99

The whole point about the Slowine, Slow Food, slow life movement is that you take time out to savour all the experiences that our existence offers us. I suppose you *could* drink this delightful pink slowly, with its strawberry and plum fruit ripeness, its apple acidity and undertow of pebbles and iron, but why not drink it fast and cold while slowly contemplating the meaning of life?

ROSÉS FOR AROUND £5

2006 Le Froglet Rosé, Vin de Pays d'Oc, Languedoc-Roussillon, France, 12% ABV
Marks & Spencer, £4.99

Froglet. How sweet. Surely this can't be the French poking mild fun at themselves? Well, Froglet turns out to be a very nice, easy pink wine with gentle pear, apple and strawberry fruit – a swig of this and they'll find it a lot easier to laugh at themselves.

nv Navarra Rosado, Agramont, Navarra, Spain, 13% ABV
Sainsbury's, £4.99

In the dark old days when most Spanish wine other than that from Rioja was pretty duff stuff, Agramont shone like a beacon for clean, tasty pinks and reds grown in the fields of Navarra. So I'm delighted to see they haven't lost their knack, and this achieves the tricky balance between ripeness, weight and freshness – lots of juicy strawberry fruit, an attractive side-swipe of acidity and the cautionary dryness of a stony riverbed in midsummer.

nv Navarra Rosado, Torre Beratxa, Navarra, Spain, 13.5% ABV
Threshers, £4.99 (3 for 2, £3.33)

Ah, Spain is so good at this style. The Garnacha grape makes marvellous, herb-strewn chunky reds, but also fresh, bright, full-flavoured yet fresh pinks, packed with apple and pear and strawberry fruit that cry out for chilling and knocking back.

2007 Rioja Rosado, Gran Familia, Bodegas Castillo de Fuenmayor, Rioja, Spain, 12% ABV
Tesco, £4.99

Rioja has been making really tasty pinks for as long as I can remember, but everyone dismisses them in the rush for red. Not me. This one is full of apple and strawberry fruit topped off with cream, and has a very lulling waxy texture too.

2006 Navarra Rosado, Malumbres, Bodegas Vicente Malumbres, Navarra, Spain, 13.5% ABV
The Wine Society, £4.95

The Garnacha grape, one of the world's most planted red grapes, makes ace rosé, both in Spain and in in southern France (as Grenache): this one's enjoyable, bright, fresh, a mellow mix of strawberry and apple and cream, with just a little stony roughness.

CHEAP AND CHEERFUL ROSÉS

2007 Los Nucos Shiraz-Cabernet Rosé, Luis Felipe Edwards, Valle Central, Chile, 13% ABV
Marks and Spencer, £3.99

Really nice basic pink wine. Both Shiraz and Cabernet are grape varieties packed with personality. They make a really punchy red combo, but can be too much of a good thing if paired up in pink. No worries. This one is well done – mild, dry, fresh, with crisp eating apple fruit given a hint of spice to kindle dreams of summer stretching from here to eternity.

2006 Tempranillo Rosé, Tierra Sana (organically grown grapes), La Mancha, Spain, 13% ABV
Co-op, £3.99

This tops the list for flavour per quid. It does have the usual apple and strawberry fruit, mellowed by cream and swirled with a little summer dust, but it also has an extra layer of fruit, of pear and melon, and a texture softened with wax.

2006 Viña Decana Rosado, Utiel-Requena, Valencia, Spain, 12.5% ABV
Aldi, £2.99

Another well-made pink from a baking hot area, this time inland from Valencia. You can taste a bit of rich date ripeness, which tells you the sun was really beating down, but they've managed to keep some bright strawberry fruit and some quite sharp apple peel acidity to nip your tonsils.

2006 Californian Charming Rosé, USA, 12.5% ABV
ASDA, £2.97

If you're after a nice, delicate, bone dry sipping pink – this isn't it. It's not delicate, it's not bone dry, it's not for sipping – but it is pink and it is nice. Pretty fruity stuff, this, partly because they've thrown in a little Muscat juice to jazz it up, and partly because the full-on Shiraz provides the bulk of the rest. Chill it right down – and it's a good drink. If you still find it a bit much – add some sparkling water and an ice cube.

Keeping it light

We're becoming increasingly disenchanted with high-alcohol wines. So, increasingly, I'm checking the alcohol content of the wines I recommend. Here are my suggestions for drinks with fab flavours, that won't leave you fuzzy-headed the next morning.

More and more wines seem to be hitting our shores at 14%, 15% – we even had a red wine in a tasting here recently that topped 16%. A red table wine! How can you enjoy that as a jolly beverage to knock back with your lamb chops: you'll be asleep or drunk before you've got the meat off the barbie.

Now, some wines have traditionally been high alcohol, and wear their strength well, but there are far too many wines that – less than a decade ago – used to perform at 11.5% to 12.5% alcohol and which are now adding at least a degree – and often more – to their strength, seemingly in an effort to ape the ripe round flavours of the New World. Thank goodness there are still a significant number showing more restraint.

At 12%–12.5% there are lots of white wines to choose from, particularly from cooler parts of France – Muscadet and Sauvignon de Touraine from the Loire and Bordeaux Blanc and Entre-Deux-Mers from Bordeaux; from northern Italy, where the most famous example is white Soave, and from numerous parts of Eastern Europe, particularly Hungary. Don't forget England too.

But we've set the bar at 12%. This cuts out most white wines from the southern hemisphere; the slightly tart, refreshing white styles that sit easily at 12% can develop better flavour at a lower strength than most reds can. This exercise reminded us that Germany is full of fantastic Riesling wines as low as 7.5%. Most supermarket house whites are 11.5–12%. Western Australia whites are often 12%. And Champagne, of all things, is only 12%. Hallelujah.

White wine

- 2006 Albariño, Tesco Finest, Rías Baixas, Galicia, Spain, £5.99, Tesco, 12% ABV
- 2005 Atlantique, Vin de Pays des Côtes de Gascogne, Sauvignon Blanc-Gros Manseng, South-West France, £4.99, Co-op, 12% ABV
- 2006 Bacchus, Chapel Down, Kent, England, £8.99, Waitrose, 11.5% ABV
- 2006 Blanc de Morgex et de la Salle, Vini Estremi, Valle d'Aosta, Italy, £9.28, les Caves de Pyrene, 11.5% ABV
- 2006 Bordeaux, Chateaux's Selection (Benoit Calvet), Sauvignon-Semillon, Bordeaux, France, £3.29, Aldi, 12% ABV (page 39)
- 2006 Chablis, Domaine Billaud-Simon, Burgundy, France, £9.95, The Wine Society, 12% ABV (page 16)
- 2006 Chablis, Vieilles Vignes, Domaine de Bieville, Burgundy, France, £10.69, Laithwaites, 12% ABV
- 2006 Château Bonnet, Les Vignobles André Lurton, Entre-Deux-Mers, Bordeaux, France, £5.99, Sainsbury's, 12% ABV (page 30)
- 2006 Chenin Blanc, Peter Lehmann, Barossa, South Australia, £5.99, Waitrose, 12% ABV
- 2006 Cape Chenin-Colombard, South Africa, £3.99, Co-op Fairtrade, 12% ABV
- 2006 Colombard-Sauvignon Blanc, La Biondina, Primo Estate, McLaren Vale, South Australia, £10.25,

Philglas & Swiggot, 12% ABV
- 2006 Cuvée Pecheur, Vin de Pays du Comté Tolosan, South-West France, £3.49, Waitrose, 11.5% ABV (page 38)
- 2007 Cuvée de Richard, Vin de Pays du Comté Tolosan, South-West France, £3.19, Majestic, 11.5% ABV (page 39)
- 2006 Dourthe No. 1, Bordeaux Sauvignon Blanc, France, £5.99, Waitrose, 12% ABV
- Flint Dry NV, Chapel Down, Kent, England, £6.99, Waitrose, 11.5% ABV
- 2006 Muscadet Côtes de Grandlieu Sur Lie, Fief Guérin, Loire Valley, France, £5.35, Waitrose, 12% ABV
- 2007 Muscadet Sèvre at Maine Sur Lie, Le Moulin de Cossardières, Loire Valley, France, £4.99, Marks & Spencer, 12% ABV
- 2006 Muscadet Sèvre et Maine, Domaine de la Tourmaline, Loire Valley, France, £5.49, Majestic, 12% ABV
- 2006 Oddbins Own White, Languedoc-Roussillon, France, £3.99, Oddbins, 12% ABV
- 2006 Domaine de Plantérieu, Vin de Pays des Côtes de Gascogne, South-West France, £4.49, Waitrose, 10.5% ABV
- 2007 Riesling, Tim Adams, Clare Valley, South Australia, £7.99, Tesco, 12% ABV (page 21)

- 2006 Riesling, Dr Bassermann-Jordan, Pfalz, Germany, £7.49, Waitrose, 11% ABV
- nv Riesling, The Best, Ewald Pfeiffer, Mosel-Saar-Ruwer, Germany, £5.99, Morrisons, 9% ABV
- 2005 Riesling, Blue Slate, Dr Loosen, Mosel, Germany, £7.99, Somerfield, 8.5% ABV
- 2006 Riesling, Boundary Road, Frankland River, Great Southern, Western Australia, £5.99, Co-op, 12% ABV
- 2005 Riesling, Eaglehawk, Wolf Blass, Australia, £5.49, Sainsbury's, 11.5% ABV (page 33)
- 2005 Riesling, Graffenreben, Alsace, France, £6.99, Waitrose, 12% ABV
- 2006 Riesling Kabinett, Ayler Kupp, Margarethenhof, Mosel, Germany, £6.99, Majestic, 9% ABV
- 2006 Riesling Kabinett, Graacher Himmelreich, Dr Loosen, Mosel, Germany, £9.99, Sainsbury's, 7.5% ABV
- 2006 Riesling Kabinett, Leitz Estate, Rüdesheim, Rheingau, Germany, £7.49, Tesco, 8.5% ABV
- 2004 Riesling Kabinett, Ürziger Würzgarten, Karl Erbes, Mosel, Germany, £7.49, Waitrose, 8% ABV
- 2005 Riesling, Rüdesheimer Berg Roseneck Old Vines, Leitz Estate, Rheingau, Germany, £17, Marks & Spencer, 8.5% ABV
- 2006 Riesling, Daniel Schuster, Waipara, New Zealand, £7.04, les Caves de Pyrene, 10.5% ABV (page 24)
- 2006 Rioja, Gran Familia, Bodegas Castillo de Fuenmayor, Rioja, Spain, £4.99, Co-op, 12% ABV
- 2007 Sauvignon Blanc, Ormonde Cellars, Darling, South Africa, £6.99, Tesco, 12% ABV (page 26)
- 2006 Sauvignon Blanc, Oxford Landing, South Australia, £6.99, widely available, 11% ABV
- 2006 Sauvignon Blanc-Semillon Reserve, Palandri Estate, Western Australia, £6.99, Co-op, 11.5% ABV
- 2006 Sauvignon Blanc-Semillon, Western Australia, £6.99, Sainsbury's Taste the difference, 12% ABV
- 2001 Semillon, Mount Pleasant Elizabeth, McWilliam's, Hunter Valley, New South Wales, Australia, £9.99, Morrisons, 11% ABV (page 15)
- 2006 Semillon, Peter Lehmann, Barossa, South Australia, £5.49, Tesco, 11.5% ABV (page 33)
- 2000 Semillon Reserve, Peter Lehmann, Barossa, South Australia, £10.99, Portland, Vin du Vin, Noel Young, 11.5% ABV
- 2006 Semillon-Sauvignon Blanc, Verse 1, Brookland Valley, Margaret River, Western Australia, £8.99, Oddbins, 12% ABV
- 2007 Semillon-Sauvignon Blanc, St Hallett Poacher's Blend, Barossa and Eden Valleys, South Australia, £7.99 (3 for 2 £5.33), Threshers, £6.99, Co-op and elsewhere, 11.5% ABV

- 2007 Soave (Organic), Veneto, Italy, £4.99, Marks & Spencer, 12% ABV
- 2006 Vin de Pays des Côtes de Gascogne, les Quatre Cépages (Colombard, Sauvignon, Ugni Blanc, Gros Manseng), Domaine de Pajot, South-West France, £4.79, Booths, Organic, 12% ABV
- 2007 Vin de Pays du Gers, South-West France, £3.49, Marks & Spencer, 11.5% ABV (page 39)
- 2006 Vin de Pays de l'Hérault, Moulin de Gassac, Mas de Daumas Gassac, Languedoc-Roussillon, France, £5.99, Averys, 12% ABV
- 2006 Vinho Verde, Quinta de Azeredo, Vino Verde, Portugal, £7.99 (3 for 2 £5.33), Threshers, £5.49 Waitrose, 11.5% ABV

- Frozé Pinotage Rosé, Western Cape, South Africa, £4.99, Co-op, Waitrose, 12% ABV
- 2006 Rioja Rosado, Gran Familia, Bodegas Castillo de Fuenmayor, Rioja, Spain, £4.99, Tesco, 12% ABV (page 47)
- 2005 Zweigelt, Langenloiser Rosé, Trocken, Bründlmayer, Kamptal, Austria, £9.99, Bacchus, Raeburn Fine Wines, Sommelier, 12% ABV (page 42)

Rosé wine

- Casablanca Rosé, Morandé, Chile, £4.99, M & S, 12% ABV
- 2006 Chapel Down English Rosé, England, £8.99, Waitrose, 11.5% ABV (page 42)
- 2005 Cheverny, Domaine Sauger, Loire Valley, France, £8.99, Flagship Wines, 12% ABV
- 2007 Le Froglet Rosé, Vin de Pays d'Oc, Languedoc-Roussillon, France, £4.99, Marks & Spencer, 12% ABV (page 46)

FIZZ

These warm summers are really are making a difference to our drinking habits. Walk through a city park any time from April to October and there are dozens of groups of people laughing, chatting, picnicking – and drinking wine. In particular fizz. I asked one park-keeper what were the empties he picked up most. He grinned and said 'Champagne'. Well, some of it may have been sparkling wine, not true Champagne. But the message was clear – we love fizz, and the longer the sun stays out, the more we'll drink of it. I haven't included most of the big-brand Champagnes here because you can get better stuff for a tenner less – that tenner would have gone on their advertising and marketing budget, not on extra quality. And, as our winners show, you don't have to be drinking Champagne to get stunning Champagne flavours.

• The wines are listed in descending price order.

BEST WHITE FIZZ

nv Champagne Brut Classic, Deutz, France, 12% ABV
Berkmann and independent retailers, £27.99

This was the best of the big-name Champagnes I tried for this book — it's not a mega-name but it's always good. This is classy stuff as usual, though it no longer has a kind of cedar scent that used to mark it out a few years ago. I'd age it another couple of years, but right now it does possess a full soft foam, crunchy fresh apple fruit and a hint of cream that will spread out in time.

Champagne Brut, Mis en Cave 2003, Charles Heidsieck,
France, 12% ABV **Booths, £26.99**

Just as good as the Deutz (above). If only the other big companies took as much care of their product as Charles Heidsieck does. Year in, year out, this is soft yet lively, dry yet creamy, its acidity charmingly matched by the softness of brioche and the scent of hazelnuts.

nv Champagne Brut, Fleury, France, 12.5% ABV
Waitrose, £24.99

This is a biodynamic wine. I won't go into all the details here, but that means the vineyards are cultivated as naturally as possible, usually in a fairly obsessive way. Which should make for super-quality fruit. Well, this champagne is certainly intense — deep loft apple and apple purée flavours, along with some apple and lemon peel acidity and a pretty rich palate. It's a mood fizz; don't choose it if you're feeling frivolous or hysterical.

2002 Vintage Champagne Brut, Oudinot, France, 12% ABV
Marks & Spencer, £21.99

When I saw the vintage, I thought, that's too young, especially in a serious vintage year like 2002. But the ripeness levels were very high in 2002 and the acid levels were rather low, so it has been possible to release a rich, yeasty, nutty wine, full of youthful foam and bright apple fruit, but mercifully low in acidity. And at six years old, it's ready.

    M&S are putting some good stuff under their Oudinot label at the moment. There is also a good non-vintage, Chardonnay-based fizz for £18.99 and, although it's fairly young, it has a lovely, gentle, soft quality, mild apple fruit rubbing shoulders with hazelnuts wrapped in a mellow coating of cream.

nv Champagne Blanc de Blancs, France, 12% ABV
Waitrose, £19.49

For years this has been one of the most elegant Champagnes on the market and it's not the first time it's been a winner for me. 'Elegant' is a tricky wine word, overused, often implying lack of oomph. But not here. This has the elegance of a BBC costume drama, of *Pride and Prejudice*, silks and crinolines and parasols. Creamy, soft, caressing your palate, wooing your senses, dismantling the barriers around your soul and teasing you to say 'why not?'

2004 Bloomsbury Cuvée Merret, Ridgeview, West Sussex, England, 12% ABV
Waitrose, Butlers Wine Cellar and other independents, £18–£19

The potential for English fizz is massive, and the producers have had a couple of stellar years, winning awards and accolades worldwide. But I feel they're slightly stretched at the moment, perhaps because, for the first time, demand has exceeded supply. Even so, this cuvée from Ridgeview is looking good – quite high in acidity, but that's not unusual with English wines and it means they age extremely well. The fruit is good strong baked apple peel – Bramleys, I should say – and there's honey and yeast there in support. Serious, lean, but good.

2002 Pelorus, Cloudy Bay, New Zealand, 12.5% ABV
Majestic, Sainsbury's and independent retailers, £17–£19

Wonderful stuff. I've been praising the non-vintage Pelorus for years, often using it in blind tastings where it triumphantly routed much more expensive and famous names from Champagne itself. And I'd half-forgotten Pelorus make a vintage wine, too, which is even better. Pelorus is the sparkling wine of Cloudy Bay in New Zealand. Cloudy Bay is owned by the same bunch as Veuve Clicquot, Moët & Chandon, all that lot. So this is sort of down-under Veuve Clicquot. Well, I hope the French guys get hold of a few bottles of this, because this has more class than their Champagne offerings, and it's way cheaper. It's fabulously creamy, it's pulsating with lively apple flesh and hazelnuts wrapped in soft yeast, and the bubbles foam and flirt around your tongue. You could age this for another five years and it would be even better – but it's also great now.

nv Champagne, Premier Cru Brut (Union Champagne), France, 12% ABV
Tesco, £14.99

Tesco sell so much of this that, despite their best efforts, you can't be quite sure that you'll get it at its absolute best. Even so, it's never worse than good, and is an impressive effort by the producers, a large co-operative group in the best Chardonnay-growing area of Champagne. This is a little leaner than sometimes but there's good young apple there, attractive acidity and a mellow yeasty cream that will soften the wine over the next few months.

2005 Vintage Cava Brut (Codorníu), Cataluña, Spain, 11.5% ABV
Sainsbury's Taste the difference, £9.99

Classy fizz made by the giant Codorníu, the world's biggest sparkling wine company, mostly from Chardonnay, so you get ripe apple fruit, soft and fresh, good yeasty cream but also an unexpected and attractive hint of green peppercorns to tone up your palate.

2006 Prosecco, Vigna Del Cuc, Case Bianche, Martino Zanetti, Veneto, Italy, 11.5% ABV
Bat & Bottle, £8.90

I can see why the Venetians drink so much Prosecco – and I'm not sure why we don't drink more. This is utterly beguiling, with soft pear and apple flesh coated in cream, a hint of floral scent – and it's not quite dry. If it were, it wouldn't be so good.

nv Bluff Hill Brut, New Zealand, 12% ABV

Marks & Spencer, £7.99

Loads of class from New Zealand for a bargain price. You'll always get intense fruit in New Zealand fizz – and Chardonnay, Sauvignon and most other things Kiwi – so they've got to keep the fruit in check as well as celebrate it. Which is exactly what they do here. There's loads of rich yeast, a nutty savoury fullness like flaked toasted nuts in muesli, but also good acid fruit and invigorating foam.

nv Cava Brut, Vineyard X (Covides), Cataluña, Spain, 11.5% ABV

Threshers, £4.99 (3 for 2, £3.33)

This has to be the party fizz – it's fresh, spicy and really quite mellow. Add a cool label and the party's already humming.

BEST ROSÉ FIZZ

nv Champagne Oudinot Rosé, France, 12% ABV
Marks & Spencer, £21.99

Another good glass from Oudinot (see also page 57), cleverly blending softness with a bit of bite. The fruit is all mild apple flesh, maybe a little squashy strawberry too, and the texture's glycerine soft; but there's a really intriguing twist of black pepper in there which gives it real character. The French sometimes drink Champagne with strawberries and a sprinkling of freshly ground black pepper. I can see it might work.

nv English Sparkling Rosé, Chapel Down, England, 12% ABV
Sainsbury's Taste the difference, £17.99

An increasing number of English sparklers are doing a brilliant job of aping Champagne by using the same soils – cretaceous chalk, the same method of production, and the same grapes – Chardonnay and Pinot Noir. This delightful fizz from Chapel Down in Kent uses just 15% Pinot Noir to add a little colour and the scent of strawberries. The bulk of the grapes are old English stalwart whites – Reichensteiner and Müller-Thurgau – and these give a bright appley fruit and a haughty stony leanness that isn't like Champagne, but is proudly, Kentishly English.

nv Cuvée Napa Rosé, Mumm, Napa Valley, California, 12.5% ABV
Sainsbury's, £11.99

Well, praise the Lord. Cuvée Napa Rosé is back on form. At last. In the early 1990s this wine led the battle against overpriced, overhyped, under-flavoured Champagnes. It then went into inexplicable decline for more than a decade. But it's back. Hallelujah. It isn't completely dry – California fizz rarely is – but it has a soft, come-hither apple flesh fruit with the oily acidity of lemon zest and just a hint of scent. And that's a good drink.

nv Jansz Rosé, Yalumba, Tasmania, Australia, 12.5% ABV
Flagship, Oddbins, Oz Wines, Philglas & Swiggot, Selfridges, Noel Young, £9.99–£10.99

Jansz is a Tasmanian outfit, originally started by Champagne house Louis Roederer and now owned by Aussie star family firm Yalumba. I use the non-vintage white Jansz in tastings all round the country every year and people love it. Well, they're going to love this new rosé even more. It's pale salmon pink, with a lovely, persistent, tiny bubble that lasts for ages in the glass if someone interrupts your drinking by trying to hold a conversation. The flavour foams and swirls round your mouth, creamy yeast mixing with pale strawberry fruit and a delightful fresh texture as soft as beeswax.

nv Crémant de Bourgogne rosé, Blason de Bourgogne, Caves de Bailly, Burgundy, France, 12% ABV **Waitrose, £8.99**

These guys at Bailly make good wine. Whenever you're after high-quality, pink fizz from France and don't want to pay a silly Champagne price – look at small print on the bottom of the label to check if the word 'Bailly' is there. Situated a few miles west of Chablis, they grow Pinot Noir and Gamay grapes that don't really ripen enough to make red table wine, but which are perfect for pink fizz – fun and dry, with a mild strawberry fruit sharpened with apple acid and then softened by creamy yeast.

nv Cabernet Rosé Brut, Ackerman, Loire Valley, France, 12% ABV **Waitrose, £6.99**

This is a nice pink fizz, particularly because you can really taste the Cabernet grapes through the bubbles. There's a delightful mild blackcurrant leaf and raspberry flavour chilled down with chalk from the riverbed, and the foam seems to aid rather than hinder the pleasure.

nv Cava Reserva Brut Rosado, Palau Gazo, Spain, 11.5% ABV
Booths, £5.49

Good blushing bubbly. It's pretty dry, has a lovely caressing foam and a really interesting flavour of ripe apple, some red plum flesh and a touch of rosehip scent.

And finally two black sparkling wines to try

2000 The Black Queen Sparkling Shiraz, Peter Lehmann, South Australia, 14% ABV **Vin du Van, £13.95**

This is one of those wines that makes me feel like the bulldog on the Churchill Insurance adverts. 'Oh yes,' I growl, give me some of that. Tasting sparkling wines can be hard work (oh yes it can) – all those bubbles and that acidity make your tonsils sore. And then you pour out this exuberant purple brew. Yes, purple. This is a great big unashamed wodge of ripe black Shiraz that has had the effrontery to add bubbles. It's a big, butch, rich blackcurrant, damson and liquorice Aussie Shiraz dressed up in a pink frothy tutu, legless with mirth. If you've not tried this uproarious happy juice, well, don't blame me, I'm telling you.

nv Sparkling Shiraz, Banrock Station, South Eastern Australia, 14% ABV **Widely available, £8.49**

This is my standby pick-me-up. You can get it all over the place for not much money. It's bursting with easygoing, syrupy plum and blackberry fruit and it makes you giggle and groan as you spill the purple foam all down your shirt. It won't come out, but what the hell.

Wine style guide

When faced with a shelf – or a screen – packed with wines from around the world, where do you start? Well, if you're after a particular flavour, my guide to wine styles will point you in the right direction.

White Wines

Bone-dry, neutral whites

Neutral wines exist for the sake of seafood or to avoid interrupting you while you're eating. It's a question of balance, rather than aromas and flavours, but there will be a bit of lemon, yeast and a mineral thrill in a good Muscadet sur lie or a proper Chablis. Loads of Italian whites do the same thing, but Italy is increasingly picking up on the global shift towards fruit flavours and maybe some oak. Basic, cheap South African whites are often a good bet if you want something thirst-quenching and easy to drink. Colombard and Chenin are fairly neutral grape varieties widely used in South Africa, often producing appley flavours, and better examples add a lick of honey.

- Muscadet
- Chenin Blanc and Colombard – from the Loire Valley, South-West France, Australia, California or South Africa
- Basic white Bordeaux and Entre-Deux-Mers
- Chablis
- Pinot Grigio

Green, tangy whites

For nerve-tingling refreshment, Sauvignon Blanc is the classic grape, full of fresh grass, gooseberry and nettle flavours. I always used to go for New Zealand versions, but I'm now more inclined to reach for an inexpensive bottle from Chile, South Africa or Hungary. Or even a simple white Bordeaux, because suddenly

Bordeaux Sauvignon is buzzing with life. Most Sancerre and the other Loire Sauvignons are overpriced. Austria's Grüner Veltliner has a peppery freshness. From north-west Iberia, Galicia's Albariño grape has a stony, mineral lemon zest sharpness; the same grape is used in Portugal, for Vinho Verde. Alternatively, look at Riesling: Australia serves it up with aggressive lime and mineral flavours, and New Zealand and Chile give milder versions of the same style. Alsace Riesling is lemony and dry, while German Rieslings go from bone-dry to intensely sweet, with the tangiest, zestiest, coming from the Mosel Valley.

- Sauvignon Blanc – from New Zealand, Chile, Hungary, South Africa, or Bordeaux
- Loire Valley Sauvignons such as Sancerre and Pouilly-Fumé
- Riesling – from Australia, Austria, Chile, Germany, New Zealand, or Alsace in France
- Austrian Grüner Veltliner
- Vinho Verde from Portugal and Albariño from north-west Spain

Drink organic – or even biodynamic

- The widely discussed benefits of organic farming – respect for the environment, minimal chemical residues in our food and drink – apply to grapes as much as to any other produce. Full-blown organic viticulture forbids the use of synthetic fertilizers, herbicides or fungicides; instead, cover crops and companion planting encourage biodiversity and natural predators to keep the soil and vines healthy. Warm, dry climates like the South of France, Chile and South Africa have the advantage of rarely suffering from the damp that can cause rot, mildew and other problems – we should be seeing more organic wines from these regions. Organic wines from European countries are often labelled 'Biologique', or simply 'Bio'.
- Biodynamic viticulture takes working with nature one stage further: work in the vineyard is planned in accordance with the movements of the planets, moon, sun and cosmic forces to achieve health and balance in the soil and in the vine. Vines are treated with infusions of mineral, animal and plant materials, applied in homeopathic quantities, with some astonishing results.
- If you want to know more, the best companies to contact are Vinceremos and Vintage Roots.

Intense, nutty whites

The best white Burgundy from the Côte d'Or cannot be bettered for its combination of soft nut and oatmeal flavours, subtle, buttery oak and firm, dry structure. Prices are often hair-raising and the cheaper wines rarely offer much Burgundy style. For £7 or £8 your best bet is oaked Chardonnay from an innovative Spanish region such as Somontano or Navarra. You'll get a nutty, creamy taste and nectarine fruit with good oak-aged white Bordeaux or traditional white Rioja. Top Chardonnays from New World countries – and Italy for that matter – can emulate Burgundy, but once again we're looking at serious prices.

- White Burgundy – including Meursault, Pouilly-Fuissé, Chassagne-Montrachet, Puligny-Montrachet
- White Bordeaux – including Pessac-Léognan, Graves
- White Rioja
- Chardonnay from New Zealand and Oregon – and top examples from Australia, California and South Africa

Ripe, tropical whites

Aussie Chardonnay conquered the world with its upfront flavours of peaches, apricots and melons, usually spiced up by the vanilla, toast and butterscotch richness of new oak. This winning style has now become a standard-issue flavour produced by all sorts of countries, though I still love the original. You'll need to spend a bit more than a fiver nowadays if you want something to relish beyond the first glass. Oaked Australian Semillon can also give rich, ripe fruit flavours, as can oaked Chenin Blanc from New Zealand and South Africa. If you see the words 'unoaked' or 'cool-climate' on an Aussie bottle, expect an altogether leaner drink.

- Chardonnay: from Australia, Chile, California
- Oak-aged Chenin Blanc from New Zealand and South Africa
- Australian Semillon

Aromatic whites

Alsace has always been a plentiful source of perfumed, dry or off-dry whites: Gewurztraminer with its rose and lychee scent or Muscat with its floral, hothouse grape perfume. A few producers in New Zealand, Australia, Chile and South Africa are having some success with these grapes. Floral, apricotty Viognier, traditionally the grape of Condrieu in the northern Rhône, now appears in vins de pays from all over southern France and also from California and Australia. Condrieu is expensive (£20 will get you entry-level stuff and no guarantee that it will be fragrant); vin de pays wines start at around £5 and are just as patchy. For aroma on a budget grab some Hungarian Irsai Olivér or Argentinian Torrontés. English white wines often have a fresh, floral hedgerow scent – the Bacchus grape is one of the leaders of this style.

- Alsace whites, especially Gewurztraminer and Muscat
- Gewürztraminer from Austria, Chile, Germany, New Zealand and cooler regions of Australia
- Condrieu, from the Rhône Valley in France
- Viognier from southern France, Argentina, Australia, California, Chile
- English white wines
- Irsai Olivér from Hungary
- Torrontés from Argentina

Finding vegetarian and vegan wine

Virtually all wine is clarified with 'fining' agents, many of which are animal by-products. Although they are not present in the finished wine, they are clearly not acceptable for strict vegetarians and vegans. Alternatives such as bentonite clay are widely used and vegan wines rely solely on these; vegetarian wines can use egg whites or milk proteins.

- **Specialist merchants** Organic specialists such as Vinceremos and Vintage Roots assess every wine on their lists for its vegetarian or vegan status.
- **Supermarkets** Most supermarkets stock some vegetarian and vegan wines and identify own-label ones with a symbol, such as the 'V' logo used by Somerfield and Marks & Spencer.
- **Other outlets** Check the labels. Some producers, such as Chapoutier, use a 'V' symbol to indicate vegetarian wines.

Rosé Wines

Good rosé is lovely stuff: dry, strawberryish, perhaps herby, and ideal for summer drinking with and without food. It should be fragrant and refreshing – a cool drink on a scorching day – and deliciously dry, not sickly and sweet. Remember to drink it young and to drink it cold. The darker the colour of the wine the stronger the flavour is likely to be and check the alcohol levels as they can be high.

Dry, gutsy rosé can be wonderful, with flavours of strawberries and maybe raspberries and rosehips, cherries, apples and herbs, too. Most countries make a dry rosé, and any red grape will do. Look for wines made from sturdy grapes like Cabernet, Syrah or Merlot, or go for Grenache/Garnacha or Tempranillo from Spain and the southern Rhône Valley. South America is a good bet for flavoursome, fruit-forward pink wine. Blush Zinfandel, which is white with just a hint of pink from California, is fairly sweet, but okay as a chilled-down drink. Other sweetish rosés come from the Loire Valley (Rosé d'Anjou) and Portugal. *Rosato* and *rosado* are the Italian and Spanish terms for rosé.

Delicate rosés

- Attractive, slightly leafy-tasting Bordeaux Rosé, usually based on Merlot. Bordeaux Clairet is a lightish red, virtually rosé but with more substance
- Cabernet d'Anjou from the Loire is a bit sweeter but tasty. Better still is Rosé de Loire, a lovely, dry wine full of red berry fruits
- Elegant Pinot Noir rosés from Sancerre in the upper Loire and Marsannay in northern Burgundy
- Dry but fruity rosés from the South of France and southern Rhône Valley (Coteaux d'Aix-en-Provence, Côtes du Lubéron and Côtes du Ventoux). Côtes de Provence is usually dry but fairly unmemorable. Bandol, Palette and Bellet are pricier versions from specific regions of Provence
- Light, slighly scented styles from the southern Rhône, in particular Costières de Nîmes
- Light, fresh pale rosé called *chiaretto*, from Bardolino and Riviera del Garda Bresciano on the shores of Lake Garda in northern Italy and from the same grapes as neighbouring Valpolicella
- Tasty Garnacha rosado from Navarra and Rioja in northern Spain

Gutsy rosés

- Big, strong, dry rosés from Tavel and Lirac in the southern Rhône that go well with food. Drink young at a year old if you want a cheerful, heady yet refreshing wine
- Robust Shiraz and Cabernet rosé from Chile and Malbec rosé from Argentina
- Dry, fairly full rosé from California, often from Syrah (not to be confused with the sweeter blush Zinfandel Californian rosés, labelled until 2008 as White Zinfandel)
- Fruity Australian Grenache from the Barossa Valley
- La Mancha and Jumilla in central, south-eastern Spain
- Puglia and Sicily in southern Italy make mouthfilling rosés
- Rosé des Riceys is still dark, pink wine from Pinot Noir in the southern part of the Champagne region. Rarely made and hard to find, tt is almost as full-bodied as a red wine

Why choose Fairtrade?

By the time you've paid duty and VAT, and the retailer has taken their profit, there's often precious little left for the producer – if you buy a bottle of wine for £4.99, the producer gets, on average, just £1.35, but sometimes much less. Fairtrade is an independent UK body that works in partnership with producers in developing countries and guarantees a fair price for their products. Money is invested to help the growers and their communities to build a better future. You can be sure your money is doing good in the communities where the wine is produced. I've visited Fairtrade operations in South Africa, Argentina and Chile, and I always encourage them to keep quality up – as long as they do, we'll keep buying their wine. www.fairtrade.org.uk

Sparkling Wines

Champagne can be the finest sparkling wine on the planet, but fizz made by the traditional Champagne method in Australia, New Zealand or California – often using the same grape varieties – is often just as good and cheaper. It might be a little more fruity, whereas Champagne concentrates on bready, yeasty or nutty aromas, but a few are dead ringers for the classic style. Fizz is also made in other parts of France: Crémant de Bourgogne is one of the best. England is beginning to show its potential. Italy's Prosecco is soft and delicately scented. Spain's Cava is perfect party fizz available at bargain basement prices.

Most sparkling wine is white but rosé is increasingly popular and is generally found wherever traditional method sparkling wine is made: the Loire Valley, Burgundy, California and Australia.

Sparkling red wine is rather an unusual proposition, but Australia has a rich, long-lived style usually based on Shiraz grapes but also from Merlot and Cabernet Sauvignon. You'll either love them or loathe them, but you haven't lived until you've given them a try.

- Champagne (the majority of Champagne is non-vintage and Brut is usually the driest style)
- Traditional method fizz made in the same way as Champagne and from the Champagne grapes (Chardonnay, Pinot Noir and Pinot Meunier) grown in Australia, California, England, New Zealand and South Africa. Many of the best are made by local subsidiaries of the French Champagne companies
- Crémant de Bourgogne, Crémant de Loire, Crémant de Jura, Crémant d'Alsace, Blanquette de Limoux, all from France
- Cava from Spain is pretty good but tends to be a bit earthy
- Light and creamy Prosecco from north-east Italy
- Sweet, scented grapy Asti from north-west Italy can be delightful; even better is the semi-sparkling version, Moscato d'Asti
- Sekt is sparkling wine from Germany and is occasionally 100 per cent Riesling
- Sparkling Shiraz – an Aussie speciality – will make a splash at a wild party
- Lambrusco from Italy is gently sparkling and usually red

Storing, serving and tasting wine

Wine is all about enjoyment, so don't let anyone make you anxious about opening, serving, tasting and storing it. Here are some tips to help you enjoy your wine all the more.

The corkscrew

The first step in tasting any wine is to extract the cork. Look for a corkscrew with an open spiral and a comfortable handle. The Screwpull brand is far and away the best, with a high-quality open spiral. 'Waiter's friend' corkscrews – the type you see used in restaurants – are good too, once you get the knack.

Corkscrews with a solid core that looks like a giant woodscrew tend to mash up delicate corks or get stuck in tough ones. And try to avoid those 'butterfly' corkscrews with the twin lever arms and a bottle opener on the end; they tend to leave cork crumbs floating in the wine.

First remove the metal foil or plastic seal around the top of the bottle, known as the capsule. Wipe the lip of the bottle with a clean cloth if there is dirt or mould around the top of the cork. Stand the bottle on a flat surface, press the point of the corkscrew gently into the centre of the cork and turn the screw slowly and steadily, keeping it straight. Try to stop turning before the point emerges at the bottom of the cork and ease the cork out gently.

Corks and other closures

Please don't be a cork snob. The only requirements for the seal on a bottle of wine are that it should be hygienic, airtight, long-lasting and removable. Cork has stood the test of time but now has serious competition. Real cork is environmentally friendly, but is prone to shrinkage, especially if the bottles are stored upright, and infection, which can taint the wine, giving it a musty taste.

Synthetic or plastic closures modelled on the traditional cork are common in budget wines and are increasingly used by high-quality producers, as are screwcaps, or Stelvin closures. The best synthetic closures have a soft texture and come in a range of bright colours. Most everyday whites and rosés now use either plastic corks or screwcaps.

Decanting

There are three reasons for putting wine in a decanter: to separate it from sediment that has formed in the bottle (this usually only happens with vintage port and mature red wine); to let it breathe (bringing the wine into contact with oxygen can open up the flavours); and to make it look attractive. You don't need to decant wine ages before serving and you don't need a special decanter: a glass jug is just as good. And there's no reason why you shouldn't decant the wine to aerate it, then pour it back into its bottle to serve it.

Temperature

The temperature of wine undoubtedly has a bearing on its flavour. It's better to serve wine slightly too cool, because you can always warm the glass in your hand. Don't do anything dramatic to change a wine's temperature: sticking the bottle in the freezer should be considered a last resort. One rule of thumb is that the cheaper the wine, the colder it should be served.

Chilling white wines makes them taste fresher, but also subdues flavours, so bear this in mind if you're splashing out on a top-quality white – don't keep it in the fridge too long. Most white wines are probably best at 10–12°C/50–54°F, which they will reach after an hour or two in the fridge. Dry, neutral whites and tangy Sauvignon Blanc wines can take more chilling: up to two or three hours in the fridge. Aromatic whites such as Riesling and Gewurztraminer start losing their perfume if you chill them for more than two hours. Rosés should always be well chilled. Champagnes and other sparkling wines must be well chilled to avoid exploding corks and fountains of foam.

For quick chilling, fill a bucket with ice and cold water, plus a few spoonfuls of salt if you're in a real hurry. This is much more effective than ice on its own. If the wine is already cool a vacuum-walled cooler will maintain the temperature.

The wine glass

The ideal wine glass is a fairly large tulip shape, made of fine, clear glass, with a slender stem. This shape helps to concentrate the aromas of the wine and to show off its colours and texture. For sparkling wine choose a tall, slender glass, as it helps the bubbles to last longer. Coloured glass will obscure the wine's colour, a shame for those lovely pink rosés. Look after your glasses carefully. Detergent residues or grease can affect the flavour of any wine and reduce the bubbliness of fizz. Ideally, wash glasses in very hot water without any detergent. Rinse thoroughly and allow to air-dry. Store upright to avoid trapping stale odours.

Keeping opened bottles

Exposure to oxygen causes wine to deteriorate. It lasts fairly well if you just push the cork back in and stick the bottle in the fridge, but you can also buy a range of effective devices to help keep oxygen at bay. Vacuvin uses a rubber stopper and a vacuum pump to remove air from the bottle. Others inject inert gas into the bottle to shield the wine from the ravages of oxidation.

Laying down wine

Most of the wines in this book are best drunk young while they are still fresh. The longer you intend to keep wine, the more important it is to store it with care. If you haven't got a cellar, find a nook – under the stairs, a built-in cupboard or a disused fireplace – that is cool, relatively dark and vibration-free, in which you can store the bottles on their sides to keep the corks moist (if a cork dries out it will let air in and spoil the wine).

Wine should be kept cool – around 10–15°C/50–55°F. It is also important to avoid sudden temperature changes or extremes: a windowless garage or outhouse may be cool in summer but may freeze in winter. Exposure to light can ruin wine, but dark bottles go some way to protecting it from light.

How to taste wine

If you just knock your wine back like a cold beer, you'll be missing most of whatever flavour it has to offer. Take a bit of time to pay attention to what you're tasting and I guarantee you'll enjoy the wine more.

Read the label

There's no law that says you have to make life hard for yourself when tasting wine. So have a look at what you're drinking and read the notes on the back label if there is one. The label will tell you the vintage, the region and/or the grape variety, the producer and the alcohol level.

Look at the wine

Pour the wine into a glass so it is a third full and tilt it against a white background so you can enjoy the range of colours in the wine. Is it dark or light? Is it viscous or watery? As you gain experience the look of the wine will tell you one or two things about the age and the likely flavour and weight of the wine. As a wine ages, whites lose their springtime greenness and gather deeper, golden hues, whereas red wines trade the purple of youth for a paler brick red.

Swirl and sniff

Give the glass a vigorous swirl to wake up the aromas in the wine, stick your nose in and inhale gently. This is where you'll be hit by the amazing range of smells a wine can produce. Interpret them in any way that means something to you personally: it's only by reacting honestly to the taste and smell of a wine that you can build up a memory bank of flavours against which to judge future wines.

Take a sip

At last! It's time to drink the wine. So take a decent-sized slurp – enough to fill your mouth about a third full. The tongue can detect only very basic flavour elements: sweetness at the tip, acidity at the sides and bitterness at the back. The real business of tasting goes on in a cavity at the back of the mouth which is really part of the nose. The idea is to get the fumes from the wine to rise up into this nasal cavity. Note the toughness, acidity and sweetness of the wine, then suck some air through the wine to help the flavours on their way. Gently 'chew' the wine and let it coat your tongue, teeth, cheeks and gums. Jot down a few notes as you form your opinion and then make the final decision… Do you like it or don't you?

Swallow or spit it out

If you are tasting a lot of wines, you will have to spit as you go if you want to remain upright and retain your judgement. Otherwise, go ahead and swallow and enjoy the lovely aftertaste of the wine.

Wine Faults

If you order wine in a restaurant and you find one of these faults you are entitled to a replacement. Many retailers will also replace a faulty bottle if you return it the day after you open it, with your receipt. Sometimes faults affect random bottles, others may ruin a whole case of wine.

- Cork taint – a horrible musty, mouldy smell indicates 'corked' wine, caused by a contaminated cork
- Volatile acidity – pronounced vinegary or acetone smells
- Oxidation – sherry-like smells are not appropriate in red and white wines
- Hydrogen sulphide – 'rotten eggs' smell.

Watchpoints

- Sediment in red wines makes for a gritty, woody mouthful. To avoid this, either decant the wine or simply pour it gently, leaving the last few centilitres of wine in the bottle.
- White crystals, or tartrates, on the cork or at the bottom of bottles of white wine are both harmless and flavourless.
- Sticky bottle neck – if wine has seeped past the cork it probably hasn't been very well kept and air might have got in. This may mean oxidized wine.
- Excess sulphur dioxide is sometimes noticeable as a smell of a recently struck match; it should dissipate after a few minutes.

Retailers' directory

All these retailers have been chosen on the basis of the quality and interest of their lists. If you want to find a local retailer, turn to the Who's Where directory on page 112. Case = 12 bottles

The following services are available where indicated:
C = cellarage G = glass hire/loan M = mail/online order T = tastings and talks

A & B Vintners

Little Tawsden, Spout Lane, Brenchley, Kent TN12 7AS (01892) 724977
fax (01892) 722673 e-mail info@abvintners.co.uk website www.abvintners.co.uk
hours Mon–Fri 9–6 cards MasterCard, Visa delivery Free 5 cases or more, otherwise £11.75 per consignment UK mainland minimum order 1 mixed case en primeur Burgundy, Languedoc, Rhône. C M T
☺ *Specialists in Burgundy, the Rhône and southern France, with a string of top-quality domaines from all three regions.*

Adnams

head office & mail order Sole Bay Brewery, Southwold, Suffolk IP18 6JW (01502) 727222
fax (01502) 727223 e-mail wines@adnams.co.uk website www.adnams.co.uk
shops Adnams Cellar & Kitchen Store, Victoria Street, Southwold, Suffolk IP18 6JW • Adnams Wine Shop, Pinkney's Lane, Southwold, Suffolk IP18 6EW • Adnams Cellar & Kitchen Store, The Old School House, Park Road, Holkham, Wells-next-the-Sea, Norfolk NR23 1AB (01328) 711714 • Adnams Cellar & Kitchen Store, Station Road, Woodbridge, Suffolk IP12 4AU (01394) 386594 • Adnams Cellar & Kitchen Store, Bath Row Warehouse, St Mary's Passage, Stamford, Lincolnshire PE9 2HG (01780) 753127 • Adnams Cellar & Kitchen Store, The Cardinal's Hat, 23 The Thoroughfare, Harleston, Norfolk IP20 9AS (01379) 854788 • Adnams Cellar & Kitchen Store, 1 Market Street, Saffron Walden, Essex CB10 1JB (01799) 527281 • Adnams Cellar & Kitchen Store, 23a Lees Yard, Off Bull Street, Holt, Norfolk NR25 6HS (01263) 715558 `
hours (Orderline) Mon–Fri 9–6.00; Cellar & Kitchen Store Southwold: Mon–Sat 9–6, Sun 11–4; Wine Shop Southwold: Mon–Sat 9.30–5.30, Sun 11–4; Holkham, Woodbridge and Stamford: Mon–Sat 10–6, Sun 11–4; Harleston: Mon–Sat 10–6; Holt: Mon–Sat 8.30–6, Sun 11–4; Hadleigh: Mon–Sat 9–6, Sun 11–4; Saffron Walden: Mon–Sat 9–7, Sun 11–4
cards Maestro, MasterCard, Visa, Delta discounts 5% for 3 cases or more, 10% for 5 cases or more delivery Free for

orders over £125 in most of mainland UK, otherwise £7.50 en primeur Bordeaux, Burgundy, Chile, Rhône, Southern France.
○ *Extensive list of personality-packed wines from around the world, chosen by Adnams' enthusiastic team of buyers.*

Aldi Stores
PO Box 26, Atherstone, Warwickshire CV9 2SH; 345 stores   store location line 08705 134262
website **www.aldi-stores.co.uk**   hours Mon–Wed 9–6, Thurs–Fri 9–7, Sat 8.30–5.30, Sun 10–4 (selected stores);
check the website for opening times of nearest store   cards Maestro, Visa (debit only).
○ *Decent everyday stuff from around the world, with lots of wines around £3.*

armit
5 Royalty Studios, 105 Lancaster Road, London W11 1QF (020) 7908 0600
fax (020) 7908 0601   e-mail **info@armit.co.uk**   website **www.armit.co.uk**   hours Mon–Fri 9–5.30
cards Maestro, MasterCard, Visa   delivery Free for orders over £250, otherwise £15 delivery charge
minimum order 1 case   en primeur Bordeaux, Burgundy, Italy, Rhône, New World. C M T
○ *Particularly strong on wines to go with food – they supply some of the country's top restaurants.*

ASDA
head office Asda House, Southbank, Great Wilson Street, Leeds LS11 5AD (0113) 243 5435
fax (0113) 241 8666   customer service (0500) 100055; 320 stores website **www.asda.co.uk**
hours Selected stores open 24 hrs, see local store for details   cards Maestro, MasterCard, Visa. T
○ *Good-value basics – lots under a fiver – and the range now includes some interesting wines at £7+.*

L'Assemblage Fine Wine Traders
Pallant Court, 10 West Pallant, Chichester, West Sussex PO19 1TG (01243) 537775
fax (01243) 538644   e-mail **sales@lassemblage.co.uk** website **www.lassemblage.co.uk**
hours Mon–Fri 9.30–6 cards Maestro, MasterCard, Visa   delivery Free for orders over £500
minimum order 1 mixed case or by arrangement   en primeur Bordeaux, Burgundy, Port, Rhône. C M T
○ *Specialist in one-off cases of fine, mature wine – great for special anniversaries.*

Averys Wine Merchants
4 High Street, Nailsea, Bristol BS48 1BT (01275) 811100
fax (01275) 811101 e-mail **sales@averys.com** website **www.averys.com**

• Shop and Cellars, 9 Culver Street, Bristol BS1 5LD (0117) 921 4146 fax (0117) 922 6318
e-mail cellars@averys.com hours Mon–Fri 9–7, Sat 9.30–5.30, Sun 10–4; Shop Mon–Sat 9–7
cards Maestro, MasterCard, Visa discounts Monthly mail order offers, Discover Wine with Averys 13th bottle free
delivery £5.99 per delivery address en primeur Bordeaux, Burgundy, Port, Rhône. C G M T
✪ A small but very respectable selection from just about everywhere in France, Italy, Spain and Germany, as well as some good New World wines.

Bacchus Wine

38 Market Place, Olney, Bucks MK46 4AJ (01234) 711140
fax (01234) 711199 e-mail wine@bacchus.co.uk website www.bacchus.co.uk
hours Mon 12–7, Tue–Fri 10.30–7, Sat 9.30–6, Sun 12–4 cards AmEx, Diners, Maestro, MasterCard, Visa
delivery £5 per dozen, local only minimum order 1 case. G M T
✪ France and Italy have the broadest coverage and you'll find many wines under £10.

Ballantynes Wine Merchants

211–17 Cathedral Road, Cardiff CF11 9PP (02920) 222202
fax (02920) 222112 e-mail richard@ballantynes.co.uk website www.ballantynes.co.uk
hours Mon–Fri 9.30–6.30, Sat 9.30–5.30 cards Access, Maestro, MasterCard, Visa discounts 8% per case
delivery £9.99 for first case; £4.99 for subsequent cases en primeur Bordeaux, Burgundy, Italy, Rhône. C G M T
✪ Italy, Burgundy, Rhône and Languedoc-Roussillon are stunning, most regions of France are well represented and there's some terrific stuff from Australia, New Zealand and Spain.

Balls Brothers

313 Cambridge Heath Road, London E2 9LQ (020) 7739 1642
fax 0870 243 9775 direct sales (020) 7739 1642 e-mail wine@ballsbrothers.co.uk
website www.ballsbrothers.co.uk hours Mon–Fri 9–5.30 cards AmEx, Diners, Maestro, MasterCard, Visa
delivery Free 1 case or more locally; £8 1 case, free 2 cases or more, England, Wales and Scottish Lowlands; islands and Scottish Highlands phone for details. G M T
✪ French specialist – you'll find something of interest from most regions – with older vintages available. Spain and Australia are also very good. Many of the wines can be enjoyed in Balls Brothers' London wine bars and restaurants.

The following services are available where indicated: **C** = cellarage **G** = glass hire/loan **M** = mail/online order **T** = tastings and talks

H & H Bancroft Wines

1 China Wharf, 29 Mill Street, London SE1 2BQ (020) 7232 5450
fax (020) 7232 5451   e-mail sales@bancroftwines.com   website www.bancroftwines.com
hours Mon–Fri 9–5.30   cards Delta, Maestro, MasterCard, Visa   discounts Negotiable
delivery £15 for 1–2 cases in mainland UK; free 3 cases or more or for an order value of £300 or more.
minimum order 1 unmixed case   en primeur Bordeaux, Burgundy, Rhône.   C M T
✪ *Bancroft are UK agents for an impressive flotilla of French winemakers: Burgundy, Rhône, Loire and some interesting wines from southern France. There is plenty of New World, too, and even wines from Slovenia.*

Bat & Bottle

office The Treehouse, 9 Ashwell Road, Oakham LE15 6QG (01572) 759735
warehouse 24d Pillings Road, Oakham LE15 6QF   fax 0870 458 2505   e-mail post@batwine.co.uk
website www.batwine.co.uk   hours Warehouse: Sat 9–2. Please call to arrange an appointment outside these hours
cards Maestro, MasterCard, Visa   delivery Free for orders over £150.   G M T
✪ *Ben and Emma Robson specialize in Italy, and in characterful wines from small producers.*

Bennetts Fine Wines

High Street, Chipping Campden, Glos GL55 6AG (01386) 840392   fax (01386) 840974
e-mail enquiries@bennettsfinewines.com   website www.bennettsfinewines.com   hours Tues–Sat 9.30–6
cards Access, Maestro, MasterCard, Visa   discounts On collected orders of 1 case or more   delivery £6 per case, minimum charge £12, free for orders over £200   en primeur Burgundy, California, Rhône, New Zealand.   G M T
✪ *Reasonable prices for high-calibre producers – there's lots to choose from at around £10. Mainly from France and Italy, but some good German, Spanish and Portuguese wines, too.*

Berkmann Wine Cellars

10–12 Brewery Road, London N7 9NH (020) 7609 4711   fax (020) 7607 0018   e-mail orders@berkmann.co.uk
• Brunel Park, Vincients Road, Bumpers Farm, Chippenham, Wiltshire SN14 6NQ (01249) 463501
fax (01249) 463502   e-mail orders.chippenham@berkmann.co.uk
• Brian Coad Wine Cellars, 41b Valley Road, Plympton, Plymouth, Devon PL7 1RF (01752) 334970   fax (01752) 346540
e-mail orders.briancoad@berkmann.co.uk
• Pagendam Pratt Wine Cellars, 16 Marston Moor Business Park, Rudgate, Tockwith, North Yorkshire YO26 7QF

(01423) 337567 fax (01423) 357568 e-mail orders@pagendampratt.co.uk
• T M Robertson Wine Cellars, Unit 12, A1 Industrial Estate, 232 Sir Harry Lauder Road, Portobello, Edinburgh EH15 2QA
(0131) 657 6390 fax (0131) 657 6389 e-mail orders@tmrobertson.co.uk
• Churchill Vintners, 401 Walsall Road, Perry Bar, Birmingham B42 1BT (0121) 356 8888
fax (0121) 356 1111 e-mail info@churchill-vintners.co.uk
website www.berkmann.co.uk hours Mon–Fri 9–5.30 cards Maestro, MasterCard, Visa
discounts £3 per unmixed case collected delivery Free for orders over £120 to UK mainland (excluding the Highlands)
minimum order 1 mixed case. C G M
✿ As the UK agent for, among others, Antinori, Maculan, Mastroberardino, Masi and Tasca d'Almerita, there are some great
Italian wines here. An incredibly diverse list including wines from Mexico, Corsica and India.

Berry Bros. & Rudd

3 St James's Street, London SW1A 1EG (020) 7396 9600
fax (020) 7396 9611 orders office 0870 900 4300 (lines open Mon–Fri 9–6) orders fax 0870 900 4301
• Berrys' Factory Outlet, Hamilton Close, Houndmills, Basingstoke, Hampshire RG21 6YB (01256) 323566
e-mail orders@bbr.com website www.bbr.com hours St James's Street: Mon–Fri 10–6, Sat 10–5; Berrys' Factory
Outlet: Mon–Fri 10–6, Sat–Sun 10–4 cards AmEx, Diners, Maestro, MasterCard, Visa discounts Variable
delivery Free for orders of £200 or more, otherwise £10 en primeur Bordeaux, Burgundy, Rhône. C G M T
✿ Classy and wide-ranging list. There's an emphasis on the classic regions of France. Berry's Own Selection is extensive,
with wines made by world-class producers.

Bibendum Wine Limited

mail order 113 Regents Park Road, London NW1 8UR (020) 7449 4120
fax (020) 7449 4121 e-mail sales@bibendum-wine.co.uk website www.bibendum-wine.co.uk
hours Mon–Fri 9–6 cards Maestro, MasterCard, Visa delivery Free throughout mainland UK for orders over £250,
otherwise £15 en primeur Bordeaux, Burgundy, New World, Rhône, Port. M T
✿ Equally strong in the Old World and the New: Huet in Vouvray and Lageder in Alto Adige are matched by d'Arenberg and
Katnook from Australia and Catena Zapata from Argentina.

Big Red Wine Company

mail order Barton Coach House, The Street, Barton Mills, Suffolk IP28 6AA (01638) 510803
e-mail sales@bigredwine.co.uk website www.bigredwine.co.uk hours Mon–Sat 9–6

cards AmEx, Delta, Maestro, Mastercard, Visa, PayPal discounts 5–15% for Wine Club members and on occasional offers; minimum £3 unmixed case discount; discounts for large orders negotiable delivery £5 per consignment for orders under £150, £10 for orders under £50, UK mainland en primeur Bordeaux, Rhône. C G M T

○ *Intelligently chosen, reliably individualistic wines from well-established growers in France. A list worth reading, full of information and provocative opinion – and they're not overcharging.*

Booths

Booths, Booths Central Office, Longridge Road, Ribbleton, Preston PR2 5BX (01772) 693800
fax (01772) 693893; 26 stores across the North of England
website www.booths.co.uk and www.booths-wine.co.uk
hours Office: Mon–Fri 8.30–5; shop hours vary cards AmEx, Electron, Maestro, MasterCard, Solo, Visa
discounts 5% off any 6 bottles. G T

○ *A list for any merchant to be proud of, never mind a supermarket. There's plenty around £5, but if you're prepared to hand over £7–9 you'll find some really interesting stuff.*

Bordeaux Index

6th Floor, 159–173 St John Street, London EC1V 4QJ (020) 7253 2110
fax (020) 7490 1955 e-mail sales@bordeauxindex.com website www.bordeauxindex.com
hours Mon–Fri 8.30–6 cards AmEx, Maestro, MasterCard, Visa, JCB (transaction fees apply)
delivery (Private sales only) free for orders over £2,000 UK mainland; others at cost minimum order £500
en primeur Bordeaux, Burgundy, Rhône, Italy. C T

○ *An extensive list for big spenders, with pages and pages of Bordeaux, including Yquem, white Burgundy and vintage Champagne. You'll also find interesting stuff from Italy, Australia and America.*

Budgens Stores

head office Musgrave House, Widewater Place, Moorhall Road, Harefield, Uxbridge, Middlesex UB9 6NS 0870 050 0158
fax 0870 050 0159, 190 stores mainly in southern England and East Anglia – for nearest store call 0800 526002
e-mail info@ budgens.co.uk website www.budgens.co.uk
hours Variable according to size and location (190 stores open 24 hours); usually Mon–Sat 8–8, Sun 10–4
cards Maestro, MasterCard, Solo, Visa.

○ *These days you can be reasonably confident of going into a Budgens store and coming out with something you'd actually like to drink, at bargain-basement prices upwards.*

The Butlers Wine Cellar

247 Queens Park Road, Brighton BN2 9XJ (01273) 698724
fax (01273) 622761 e-mail henry@butlers-winecellar.co.uk website www.butlers-winecellar.co.uk
hours Tue–Sat 11–7 cards Access, AmEx, Maestro, MasterCard, Visa delivery Free locally 1 case or more; free UK mainland 3 cases or more en primeur Bordeaux. G M T
○ *Henry Butler personally chooses all the wines on the regular list and there is some fascinating stuff there, including English wines from local growers such as Breaky Bottom and Ridgeview. The rosés include English fizz and a delicious wine from Bonny Doon in California. Check the website or join the mailing list as offers change regularly.*

Anthony Byrne

mail order Ramsey Business Park, Stocking Fen Road, Ramsey, Cambs PE26 2UR (01487) 814555
fax (01487) 814962 e-mail anthony@abfw.co.uk or gary@abfw.co.uk website www.abfw.co.uk
hours Mon–Fri 9–5.30 cards MasterCard, Visa discounts Available on cases delivery Free 5 cases or more, or orders of £250 or more; otherwise £12 minimum order 1 case en primeur Bordeaux, Burgundy, Rhône. C M T
○ *A serious range of Burgundy; smaller but focused lists from Bordeaux and the Rhône; carefully selected wines from Alsace, Loire and Provence; and a wide range of New World.*

D Byrne & Co

Victoria Buildings, 12 King Street, Clitheroe, Lancashire BB7 2EP (01200) 423152
hours Mon–Sat 8.30–6 cards Maestro, MasterCard, Visa delivery Free within 50 miles; nationally £20 1st case, £5 subsequent cases en primeur Bordeaux, Burgundy, Rhône, Germany. G M T
○ *One of northern England's best wine merchants, with a hugely impressive range. Mature clarets, stacks of Burgundy, faultless Loire and Rhône, and many, many more, both Old and New World. I urge you to go see for yourself.*

Cape Wine and Food

77 Laleham Road, Staines, Middlesex TW18 2EA (01784) 451860
fax (01784) 469267 e-mail ross@capewineandfood.com website www.capewineandfood.com
hours Mon–Sat 10–6, Sun 10–5 cards Maestro, MasterCard, Visa discounts 10% mixed case. G M T
○ *If you're looking for South African wine, this shop is the place to visit. Alongside wines for everyday drinking, there are some of the Cape's top red blends, going up to around £50 a bottle.*

The following services are available where indicated: **C** = cellarage **G** = glass hire/loan **M** = mail/online order **T** = tastings and talks

Les Caves de Pyrene

Pew Corner, Old Portsmouth Road, Artington, Guildford GU3 1LP (office) (01483) 538820 (shop) (01483) 554750
fax (01483) 455068 e-mail sales@lescaves.co.uk website www.lescaves.co.uk
hours Mon–Fri 9–5 cards Maestro, MasterCard, Visa delivery Free for orders over £180 within M25, elsewhere
at cost discounts Negotiable minimum order 1 mixed case en primeur South-West France. G M T
☺ *Excellent operation, devoted to seeking out top wines from all over southern France. Other areas of France are looking
increasingly good too, Italy's regions are well represented, and there's some choice stuff from New Zealand.*

ChateauOnline

mail order BP68, 39602 Arbois Cedex, France (0033) 3 84 66 42 21
fax (0033) 1 55 30 31 41 customer service 0800 169 2736 website www.chateauonline.com
hours Mon–Fri 8–11.30, 12.30–4.30 cards AmEx, Maestro, MasterCard, Visa
delivery £7.99 per consignment en primeur Bordeaux, Burgundy, Languedoc-Roussillon.
☺ *French specialist, with an impressive list of over 2000 wines. Easy-to-use website with a well-thought-out range
of mixed cases, frequent special offers and bin end sales.*

Cockburns of Leith

Cockburn House, Unit 3, Abbeyhill Industrial Estate, Abbey Lane, Edinburgh EH8 8HL (0131) 661 8400
fax (0131) 661 7333 e-mail sales@cockburnsofleith.co.uk
website www.cockburnsofleith.co.uk hours Mon–Fri 9–6; Sat 10–5 cards Maestro, MasterCard, Visa
delivery Free 12 or more bottles within Edinburgh; elsewhere £7 1–2 cases, free 3 cases or more
en primeur Bordeaux, Burgundy. G T
☺ *Clarets at bargain prices – in fact wines from all over France, including plenty of vins de pays. Among other countries
New Zealand looks promising, and there's a great range of sherries.*

Connolly's Wine Merchants

Arch 13, 220 Livery Street, Birmingham B3 1EU (0121) 236 9269/3837
fax (0121) 233 2339 e-mail sales@connollyswine.co.uk website www.connollyswine.co.uk
hours Mon–Fri 9–5.30, Sat 10–4 cards AmEx, Maestro, MasterCard, Visa
delivery Surcharge outside Birmingham area discounts 10% for cash & carry en primeur Burgundy. G M T
☺ *There's something for everyone here. Burgundy, Bordeaux and the Rhône all look very good; and there are top names
from Germany, Italy, Spain and California. Monthly tutored tastings and winemaker dinners.*

The Co-operative Group

head office New Century House, Manchester M60 4ES Freephone 0800 068 6727 for stock details; approx. 3,000 licensed stores e-mail customer_relations@co-op.co.uk website www.co-operative.co.uk hours Variable cards Variable

☺ *Champions of Fairtrade wines. Tasty stuff from South Africa, Australia, Chile and Argentina for around £5.*

Corney & Barrow

head office No. 1 Thomas More Street, London E1W 1YZ (020) 7265 2400 fax (020) 7265 2539

• Corney & Barrow East Anglia, Belvoir House, High Street, Newmarket CB8 8DH (01638) 600000

• Corney & Barrow (Scotland) with Whighams of Ayr, 8 Academy Street, Ayr KA7 1HT (01292) 267000, and Oxenfoord Castle, by Pathhead, Mid Lothian EH37 5UD (01875) 321921

e-mail wine@corbar.co.uk website www.corneyandbarrow.com hours Mon–Fri 8–6 (24-hr answering machine); Newmarket Mon–Sat 9–6; Edinburgh Mon–Fri 9–6; Ayr Mon–Fri 9–6, Sat 9.30–5.30 cards AmEx, Maestro, MasterCard, Visa delivery Free for all orders above £200 within mainland UK, otherwise £9 + VAT per delivery. For Scotland and East Anglia, please contact the relevant office en primeur Bordeaux, Burgundy, Champagne, Rhône, Italy, Spain. C G M T

☺ *Top names in French and other European wines; Australia, South Africa and South America also impressive. Wines in every price bracket – try them out at Corney & Barrow wine bars in London.*

Croque-en-Bouche

Groom's Cottage, Underdown, Gloucester Road, Ledbury HR8 2JE (01531) 636400

fax 08707 066282 e-mail mail@croque-en-bouche.co.uk website www.croque-en-bouche.co.uk hours By appointment 7 days a week cards MasterCard, Visa, debit cards discounts 3% for orders over £500 if paid by cheque or debit card delivery Free locally; elsewhere £5 per consignment; free in England and Wales for orders over £500 if paid by credit card minimum order 1 mixed case (12 items) or £180 M

☺ *A wonderful list, including older wines. Mature Australian reds from the 1990s; terrific stuff from the Rhône; some top clarets; and a generous sprinkling from other parts of the world.*

DeFINE Food & Wine

Chester Road, Sandiway, Cheshire CW8 2NH (01606) 882101

fax (01606) 888407 e-mail office@definefoodandwine.com website www.definefoodandwine.com hours Mon–Sat 10–8; Sun 12–6 cards AmEx, Maestro, MasterCard, Visa discounts 5% off 12 bottles or more delivery Free locally, otherwise £10 UK minimum order 1 mixed case. C G M T

☺ *Wine shop and delicatessen, with British cheeses and handmade pies and food specialities from Italy and Spain. Excellent, wide-ranging list of over 1000 wines including plenty of New World wines, as well as European classics.*

Devigne Wines

211 The Murrays, Edinburgh EH17 8UN (0131) 664 9058
Fax (05600) 756 287 e-mail info@devignewines.co.uk website www.devignewines.co.uk hours Mon–Fri 10–6 (telephone 7 days) cards Maestro, MasterCard, Visa discounts Selected mixed cases at introductory rate delivery Free for orders over £300, otherwise £6.50 per consignment M
☺ *Small list specializing in French wine: traditional-method sparkling wines from all over France, a wide choice of rosés, Gaillac from the South-West and wines from the Languedoc and the Jura.*

Direct Wine Shipments

5–7 Corporation Square, Belfast, Northern Ireland BT1 3AJ (028) 9050 8000
fax (028) 9050 8004 e-mail shop@directwine.co.uk website www.directwine.co.uk
hours Mon–Fri 9–6.30 (Thur 10–8), Sat 9.30–5.30 cards Access, Maestro, MasterCard, Visa discounts 10% in the form of complementary wine with each case delivery Free Northern Ireland 1 case or more, variable delivery charge for UK mainland depending on customer spend en primeur Bordeaux, Burgundy, Rhône. C M T
☺ *Rhône, Spain, Australia and Burgundy outstanding; Italy, Germany and Chile not far behind; there's good stuff from pretty much everywhere. Wine courses, tastings and expert advice offered.*

Nick Dobson Wines

38 Crail Close, Wokingham, Berkshire RG41 2PZ 0800 849 3078
fax 0870 460 2358 e-mail nick.dobson@nickdobsonwines.co.uk website www.nickdobsonwines.co.uk
hours Mon–Sat 9–5 cards Access, Maestro, MasterCard, Visa delivery £7.50 + VAT 1 case; £4.80 + VAT 2nd case and subsequent cases to UK mainland addresses. Free local delivery. M T
☺ *Mail order outfit specializing in wines from Switzerland, Austria and Beaujolais. Burgundy, Germany and New Zealand are also covered in this list. Plenty of wines at under £10.*

Domaine Direct

8 Cynthia Street, London N1 9JF (020) 7837 1142
fax (020) 7837 8605 e-mail mail@domainedirect.co.uk website www.domainedirect.co.uk
hours 8.30–6 or answering machine cards Maestro, MasterCard, Visa delivery Free London; elsewhere in UK mainland

1 case £12, 2 cases £16.90, or more free minimum order 1 mixed case en primeur Burgundy. M T

☺ *Sensational Burgundy list; prices are very reasonable for the quality. Also the Burgundian-style Chardonnays from Australia's Leeuwin Estate.*

Farr Vintners

220 Queenstown Road, Battersea, London SW8 4LP (020) 7821 2000

fax (020) 7821 2020 e-mail sales@farrvintners.com website www.farrvintners.com

hours Mon–Fri 10–6 cards Access, Maestro, Mastercard, Visa delivery London £1 per case (min £14); elsewhere at cost minimum order £500 + VAT en primeur Bordeaux. C M T

☺ *A fantastic list of the world's finest wines. The majority is Bordeaux, but you'll also find top stuff and older vintages of white Burgundy, red Rhône, plus Italy, Australia and California.*

Fine Wines of New Zealand

mail order (020) 7482 0093 fax (020) 7267 8400 e-mail sales@fwnz.co.uk or info@fwnz.co.uk website www.fwnz.co.uk (to place an order contact Catchpole & Froggitt freephone 0800 0856186 or www.pullthecork.com) hours Mon–Fri 9–6 cards Access, Maestro, MasterCard, Visa delivery £6.95 for 1 case or more UK mainland, £9.95 for 2 cases or more minimum order 1 case. M

☺ *There are some great names from New Zealand, including Ata Rangi, Redwood Valley, Pegasus Bay and Stonyridge.*

Irma Fingal-Rock

64 Monnow Street, Monmouth NP25 3EN

tel & fax 01600 712372 e-mail tom@pinotnoir.co.uk website www.pinotnoir.co.uk

hours Mon 9.30–1.30, Thurs & Fri 9.30–5.30, Sat 9.30–5 cards Maestro, Visa discounts 5% for at least 12 bottles collected from shop, 7.5% for collected orders over £500, 10% for collected orders over £1,200 delivery Free locally (within 30 miles); orders further afield free if over £100. G M T

☺ *The list's great strength is Burgundy, from some very good growers and priced between £6 and £40. Small but tempting selections from other French regions, as well as Italy, Spain, Portugal and the New World.*

Flagship Wines

417 Hatfield Road, St Albans, Hertfordshire AL4 0XP (01727) 865309 e-mail sales@flagshipwines.co.uk website www.flagshipwines.co.uk hours Tues–Thurs 11–6, Fri 11–7.30, Sat 10–6 cards AmEx, Maestro, MasterCard,

Visa delivery Free to St Albans addresses and £8 to other UK mainland addresses. G M T

✪ *Well-run independent whose prices can match those of the supermarkets – and you get the friendly, well-informed advice of boss Julia Jenkins thrown in. Some interesting Italians but strongest in Spain, Australia and Portugal.*

Le Fleming Wines

mail order 19 Spenser Road, Harpenden, Hertfordshire AL5 5NW (01582) 760125
e-mail cherry@ leflemingwines.co.uk website www.leflemingwines.co.uk hours 24-hour answering machine
discounts 5% on large orders delivery Free locally minimum order 1 case. G

✪ *Mainly New World and France, alongside excellent Australian and South African. List also includes short, focused selections from Italy and Spain.*

The Flying Corkscrew

Leighton Buzzard Road, Water End, Nr Hemel Hempstead, Hertfordshire HP1 3BD (01442) 412311
fax (01442) 412313 e-mail sales@flyingcorkscrew.co.uk website www.flyingcorkscrew.co.uk
hours Mon–Wed 10–7, Thurs–Fri 10–8, Sat 10–7, Sun 11–5 cards AmEx, Maestro, MasterCard, Visa
discounts 10% on case delivery Free for orders over £100; £10 per case under £100. G M T

✪ *The list is overflowing with an extensive and imaginative range of wines from every corner of France. Italy, Australia and the US are terrific. Friendly, knowledgeable staff – and if you're local, look out for tastings led by experts and winemakers.*

Fortnum & Mason

181 Piccadilly, London W1A 1ER (020) 7734 8040
fax (020) 7437 3278 ordering line 0845 300 1707 e-mail info@fortnumandmason.co.uk
website www.fortnumandmason.com hours Mon–Sat 10–6.30, Sun 12–6 (Food Hall and Patio Restaurant only)
cards AmEx, Diners, Maestro, MasterCard, Visa discounts 1 free bottle per unmixed dozen
delivery £7 per delivery address en primeur Bordeaux. M T

✪ *Impressive names from just about everywhere, including Champagne, Bordeaux, Burgundy, Italy, Germany, Australia, New Zealand, South Africa and California. Impeccably sourced own-label range.*

Friarwood

26 New King's Road, London SW6 4ST (020) 7736 2628 fax (020) 7731 0411
• 16 Dock Street, Leith, Edinburgh, EH6 6EY (0131) 554 4159 fax (0131) 554 6703 e-mail sales@friarwood.com;

edinburgh@friarwood.com website www.friarwood.com hours Mon–Sat 10–7
cards AmEx, Diners, Maestro, MasterCard, Visa, Solo, Electron discounts 5% on mixed cases, 10% unmixed
delivery (London) Free within M25 and on orders over £250 in mainland UK; (Edinburgh) free locally and for 2 cases or
more elsewhere (under 2 cases at cost) en primeur Bordeaux. C G M T
✪ *The focus is Bordeaux, including mature wines from a good selection of petits châteaux as well as classed growths.*
Burgundy and other French regions are strong too.

Gauntleys

4 High Street, Exchange Arcade, Nottingham NG1 2ET (0115) 911 0555
fax (0115) 911 0557 e-mail rhone@gauntleywine.com website www.gauntleywine.com
hours Mon–Sat 9–5.30 cards Maestro, MasterCard, Visa delivery Free within Nottingham area, otherwise 1–3 cases
£9.50, 4 or more cases free minimum order 1 case en primeur Alsace, Burgundy, Italy, Loire, Rhône, southern France,
Spain. M T
✪ *They've won awards for their Rhône and Alsace lists. The Loire, Burgundy, southern France and Spain are also excellent.*

Goedhuis & Co

6 Rudolf Place, Miles Street, London SW8 1RP (020) 7793 7900
fax (020) 7793 7170 e-mail sales@goedhuis.com website www.goedhuis.com
hours Mon–Fri 9–5.30 cards Maestro, MasterCard, Visa delivery Free 3 cases or more, otherwise £15 England,
elsewhere at cost minimum order 1 unmixed case en primeur Bordeaux, Burgundy, Rhône. C G M T
✪ *Fine wine specialist. Bordeaux, Burgundy and the Rhône are the core of the list, but everything is good.*

Great Northern Wine

The Warehouse, Blossomgate, Ripon, North Yorkshire HG4 2AJ (01765) 606767
fax (01765) 609151 e-mail info@greatnorthernwine.co.uk website www.greatnorthernwine.co.uk
hours Tues–Fri 9–6, Sat 9–5.30 cards AmEx, Maestro, MasterCard, Visa discounts 10% on case quantities
delivery Free locally, elsewhere at cost en primeur Bordeaux. G M T
✪ *Particular strengths here are Spain, New Zealand and South America.*

Great Western Wine

The Wine Warehouse, Wells Road, Bath BA2 3AP (01225) 322810 (shop) or (01225) 322800 (office)
fax (01225) 442139 e-mail wine@greatwesternwine.co.uk website www.greatwesternwine.co.uk

hours Mon–Fri 10–7, Sat 10–6   cards AmEx, Maestro, MasterCard, Visa   discounts Negotiable   delivery £8.95 per case, free over £200   minimum order 1 mixed case   en primeur Australia, Bordeaux, Burgundy, Rioja.   C G M T
☼ *Wide-ranging list, bringing in wines from individual growers around the world. Also organizes events and tastings.*

Peter Green & Co
37A/B Warrender Park Road, Edinburgh EH9 1HJ (0131) 229 5925
fax (0131) 229 0606   e-mail shop@petergreenwines.com   hours Tues–Thur 10–6.30, Fri 10–7.30, Sat 10–6.30
cards Maestro, MasterCard, Visa   discounts 5% on unmixed half-dozens   delivery Free in Edinburgh
minimum order (For delivery) 1 case.   G T
☼ *Extensive and adventurous list: Tunisia, India and the Lebanon rub shoulders with France, Italy and Germany.*

Green & Blue
36–38 Lordship Lane, East Dulwich, London, SE22 8HJ (020) 8693 9250
• 20–26 Bedford Road, Clapham, London SW4 7HJ (020) 7498 9648
fax (020) 8693 9260   e-mail info@greenandbluewines.com   website www.greenandbluewines.com
hours Dulwich shop: Mon–Fri 10–10, Sat 9–11, Sun 12–10; Dulwich bar: Mon–Sat 9–12, Sun 12–11; Clapham
Mon–Thur 7–11, Fri 7–1, Sat 9–1, Sun 11–11pm   cards Delta, Maestro, MasterCard, Visa
discounts 5% on mixed cases and 10% on unmixed cases (for collection only)   delivery G T Free locally over £75,
otherwise £15; outside London dependent on weight, £10 under £150.   G T
☼ *A tempting list full of unusual, intriguing wines you really want to drink – and you can try them on the spot, in the wine bar, which serves tapas-style food. The staff are knowledgeable, and there's a waiting list for the popular tutored tastings. A new shop attached to the Clapham bar opened in spring 2008.*

Halifax Wine Company
18 Prescott Street, Halifax, West Yorkshire HX1 2LG (01422) 256333
e-mail andy@halifaxwinecompany.com   website www.halifaxwinecompany.com   hours Tues–Fri 9.30–6, Sat 9–5.
Closed first week in January and first week in August.   cards Access, Maestro, MasterCard, Visa   discounts 8% on 12
bottles or more for personal callers to the shop   delivery Free in West Yorkshire on orders over £75; rest of UK mainland
£9.95 for first 12 bottles then £4.95 per subsequent case.   G M T
☼ *Exciting, wide-ranging and award-winning list.*

The following services are available where indicated: **C** = cellarage **G** = glass hire/loan **M** = mail/online order **T** = tastings and talks

Handford Wines

105 Old Brompton Road, South Kensington, London SW7 3LE (020) 7589 6113 fax (020) 7581 2983
e-mail jack@handford.net website www.handford.net hours Mon–Sat 10–8.30 cards AmEx, MasterCard, Visa
discounts 5% on mixed cases delivery £8.25 for orders under £150 within UK en primeur Bordeaux. G M T
✪ *Delightful London shop, absolutely packed with the sort of wines I really want to drink.*

Roger Harris Wines

Loke Farm, Weston Longville, Norfolk NR9 5LG (01603) 880171
fax (01603) 880291 e-mail sales@rogerharriswines.co.uk website www.rogerharris wines.co.uk
hours Mon–Fri 9–5 cards AmEx, MasterCard, Visa delivery Next working day UK mainland, £3 for orders up to £110, £2
up to £160, free over £160 minimum order 1 mixed case. M
✪ *Britain's acknowledged experts in Beaujolais also have a good range of whites from the neighbouring Mâconnais region.*

Harvey Nichols

109–125 Knightsbridge, London SW1X 7RJ (020) 7235 5000
• The Mailbox, 31–32 Wharfside Street, Birmingham B1 1RE (0121) 616 6000
• 30–34 St Andrew Square, Edinburgh EH2 2AD (0131) 524 8388
• 107–111 Briggate, Leeds LS1 6AZ (0113) 204 8888
• 21 New Cathedral Street, Manchester M1 1AD (0161) 828 8888
e-mail wineshop@harveynichols.com website www.harveynichols.com
hours (London) Mon–Fri 10–8, Sat 10–7, Sun 12–6; (Birmingham) Mon–Wed 10–6, Thurs 10–8, Fri–Sat 10–7, Sun
11–5; (Edinburgh) Mon–Wed 10–6, Thurs 10–8, Fri, Sat 10–7, Sun 11–5; (Leeds) Mon–Wed 10–6, Thurs–Fri 10–7, Sat
9–7, Sun 12–6; (Manchester) Mon, Wed, Fri 10–7, Thurs 10–8, Sat 9–7, Sun 12–6
cards AmEx, Maestro, MasterCard, Visa.
✪ *Sought-after producers and cult fine wines, especially from France, Italy and California.*

Haynes Hanson & Clark

Sheep Street, Stow-on-the-Wold, Gloucestershire GL54 1AA (01451) 870808 fax (01451) 870508
• 7 Elystan Street, London SW3 3NT (020) 7584 7927 fax (020) 7584 7967
e-mail stow@hhandc.co.uk or london@hhandc.co.uk website www.hhandc.co.uk
hours (Stow) Mon–Fri 9–6, Sat 9–5.30 (London) Mon–Fri 9–7, Sat 9–4.30 cards Access, Maestro, MasterCard, Visa
discounts 10% unsplit case delivery Free central London and Gloucestershire for 1 case or more; elsewhere 1 case

£14.50, 2–3 cases £8.90 per case, 4 or more cases £7.25 per case, free orders for over £650
en primeur Bordeaux, Burgundy. M T
✪ *Known for its subtle, elegant wines: top-notch Burgundy is the main focus of the list, but other French regions are well represented, and there's interesting stuff from Spain, Italy, Australia and New Zealand.*

Hedley Wright
11 Twyford Centre, London Road, Bishop's Stortford, Herts CM23 3YT (01279) 465818 fax (01279) 465819
• Wyevale Garden Centre, Cambridge Road, Hitchin, Herts, SG4 0JT (01462) 431110 fax (01462) 422983
e-mail sales@hedleywright.co.uk website www.hedleywright.co.uk hours Mon–Wed 9–6, Thur–Fri 9–7, Sat 10–6; (Hitchin) Mon–Wed 11–7, Thur–Fri 11–8, Sat 11–7, Sun 11–5 cards AmEx, Maestro, MasterCard, Visa delivery £5 per delivery, free for orders over £100 minimum order 1 mixed case en primeur Bordeaux, Chile, Germany, Port. C G M T
✪ *A good all-round list, especially strong on France and Italy.*

Hicks & Don
4 Old Station Yard, Edington, Westbury, Wiltshire BA13 4NT (01380) 831234 fax (01380) 831010
• Park House, North Elmham, Dereham, Norfolk NR20 5JY (01362) 668571 fax (01362) 668573
e-mail mailbox@hicksanddon.co.uk website www.hicksanddon.co.uk hours Mon–Fri 9–5
cards Maestro, MasterCard, Visa discounts Negotiable delivery Free over £100, otherwise £6 per case
minimum order 1 case en primeur Bordeaux, Burgundy, Chile, Italy, Port, Rhône. C G M T
✪ *Subtle, well-made wines that go with food and plenty of good-value wines at around £6 for everyday drinking.*

Jeroboams (incorporating Laytons)
head office 7–9 Elliot's Place, London N1 8HX (020) 7288 8888 fax (020) 7359 2616
shops 50–52 Elizabeth Street, London SW1W 9PB (020) 7730 8108
• 20 Davies Street, London W1K 3DT (020) 7499 1015
• 96 Holland Park Avenue, London W11 3RB (020) 7727 9359
• 6 Pont Street, London SW1X 9EL (020) 7235 1612
• 29 Heath Street, London NW3 6TR (020) 7435 6845
• 56 Walton Street, London SW3 1RB (020) 7589 2020
• 1 St. John's Wood High Street, London NW8 7NG (020) 7722 4020
• 13 Elgin Crescent, London W11 2JA (020) 7229 0527
• Mr Christian's Delicatessen, 11 Elgin Crescent, London W11 2JA (020) 7229 0501

- Milroy's of Soho, 3 Greek Street, London W1D 4NX (020) 7437 2385 (whisky and wine)
e-mail sales@jeroboams.co.uk   website www.jeroboams.co.uk
hours Offices Mon–Fri 9–6, shops Mon–Sat 9–7 (may vary)   cards AmEx, Maestro, MasterCard, Visa
delivery Free delivery for orders over £200, otherwise £9.95   en primeur Bordeaux, Burgundy, Rhône.   C G M T
✿ *Concentrates on Burgundy, Rhône, Italy and Australia. Affordable and enjoyable wines. A wide range of fine foods, especially cheeses and olive oils, is available in the shops.*

S H Jones

27 High Street, Banbury, Oxfordshire OX16 5EW (01295) 251179   fax (01295) 272352   e-mail banbury@shjones.com
- 9 Market Square, Bicester, Oxfordshire OX26 6AA (01869) 322448   e-mail bicester@shjones.com
- The Cellar Shop, 2 Riverside, Tramway Road, Banbury, Oxfordshire OX16 5TU (01295) 672296   fax (01295) 259560
e-mail retail@shjones.com
- 121 Regent Street, Leamington Spa, Warwickshire CV32 4NU (01926) 315609   e-mail leamington@shjones.com
website www.shjones.com   hours Please call each store for details   cards Maestro, MasterCard, Visa
delivery Free for 12 bottles of wine/spirits or total value over £100 within 15-mile radius of shops, otherwise £9.75 per case   en primeur Bordeaux, Burgundy, Port.   C G M T
✿ *Wide-ranging list with good Burgundies and Rhônes, clarets from under a tenner to top names and plenty of tasty stuff from elsewhere – southern France to South America. There is now a wine bar at the High Street shop in Banbury.*

Justerini & Brooks

mail order 61 St James's Street, London SW1A 1LZ (020) 7484 6400   fax (020) 7484 6499
e-mail justorders@justerinis.com   website www.justerinis.com   hours Mon–Fri 9–5.30
cards AmEx, Maestro, MasterCard, Visa   delivery Free for unmixed cases over £250, otherwise £15 UK mainland
minimum order 1 case   en primeur Bordeaux, Burgundy, Italy, Rhône, Germany.   C M T
✿ *Superb list of top-quality wines from Europe's classic regions, as well as some excellent New World choices. While some wines are very pricy, there is plenty for less than a tenner*

Laithwaites

mail order New Aquitaine House, Exeter Way, Theale, Reading, Berkshire RG7 4PL   order line 0845 444 8282
fax 0870 444 8182   e-mail orders@laithwaites.co.uk   website www.laithwaites.co.uk   hours Mon–Fri 8–11, Sat–Sun

The following services are available where indicated: C = cellarage **G** = glass hire/loan **M** = mail/online order **T** = tastings and talks

8–9 cards AmEx, Diners, Maestro, MasterCard, Visa discounts On unmixed cases of 6 or 12 delivery £5.99 per order en primeur Australia, Bordeaux, Burgundy, Rhône, Rioja. C M T

☼ *Extensive selection of wines from France, Australia, Spain, Italy and elsewhere. Informative website offers excellent mixed cases, while the bin ends and special offers are good value.*

Lay & Wheeler

Holton Park, Holton St Mary, Suffolk CO7 6NN 0845 330 1855 fax 0845 330 4095
e-mail sales@laywheeler.com website www.laywheeler.com
hours (Order office) Mon–Fri 8.30–5.30, Sat 9–1 cards Maestro, MasterCard, Visa delivery £9.95; free for orders over £200 en primeur Bordeaux, Burgundy, Port (some vintages), Rhône, Spain. C M T
• Wheeler Cellars, 117 Gosbecks Park, Colchester, Essex CO2 9JJ (01206) 713560 fax (01206) 769552
e-mail wheeler.cellars@laywheeler.com C G M T

☼ *There's enough first-class Bordeaux and Burgundy to satisfy the most demanding drinker, and plenty more besides. A must-have list – and if you can't make up your mind they do excellent mixed cases.*

Laymont & Shaw

The Old Chapel, Millpool, Truro, Cornwall TR1 1EX (01872) 270545 fax (01872) 223005
e-mail info@laymont-shaw.co.uk website www.laymont-shaw.co.uk hours Mon–Fri 9–5 cards Maestro, MasterCard, Visa discounts £5 per case if wines collected, also £1 per case for 2 cases, £2 for 3–5, £3 for 6 or more delivery Free UK mainland minimum order 1 mixed case. C G M T

☼ *Excellent, knowledgeable list that specializes in Spain, with something from just about every region.*

Lea & Sandeman

170 Fulham Road, London SW10 9PR (020) 7244 0522 fax (020) 7244 0533
• 211 Kensington Church Street, London W8 7LX (020) 7221 1982
• 51 High Street, Barnes, London SW13 9LN (020) 8878 8643 e-mail info@leaandsandeman.co.uk
website www.londonfinewine.co.uk hours Mon–Sat 10–8 cards AmEx, Maestro, MasterCard, Visa discounts 5–15% by case, other discounts on 10 cases or more delivery London £10 for less than £100, otherwise free, and to UK mainland south of Perth on orders over £250 en primeur Bordeaux, Burgundy, Italy. C G M T

☼ *Burgundy and Italy take precedence here, and there's a succession of excellent names, chosen with great care. Bordeaux has wines at all price levels, and there are short but fascinating ranges from the USA, Spain, Australia and New Zealand.*

Liberty Wines

mail order Unit D18, New Covent Garden Food Market, London SW8 5LL (020) 7720 5350
fax (020) 7720 6158 website www.libertywine.co.uk e-mail info@libertywine.co.uk hours Mon–Fri 9–5.30
cards Maestro, MasterCard, Visa delivery Free to mainland UK minimum order 1 mixed case. M
✪ *Italy rules, with superb wines from pretty well all the best producers. Liberty are the UK agents for most of their producers, so if you're interested in Italian wines, this should be your first port of call. Also top names from Australia and elsewhere.*

Linlithgow Wines

Crossford, Station Road, Linlithgow, West Lothian EH49 6BW tel & fax (01506) 848821
e-mail jrobmcd@aol.com hours Mon–Fri 9–5.30 (please phone first) cards None: cash, cheque or bank transfer only delivery Free locally; elsewhere in UK £6.50 for 1 case, £4.75 per case for 2 or more. G M T
✪ *Specialist in the south of France – Languedoc, southern Rhône and Provence – with lots around £5–7; prices rarely exceed £20.*

O W Loeb & Co

3 Archie Street, off Tanner Street, London SE1 3JT (020) 7234 0385
fax (020) 7357 0440 e-mail finewine@owloeb.com website www.owloeb.com hours Mon–Fri 8.30–5.30
cards Maestro, MasterCard, Visa discounts 3 cases and above delivery Free 3 cases or more and on orders over £250
minimum order 1 case en primeur Burgundy, Bordeaux, Rhône, Germany (Mosel). C M T
✪ *Burgundy, the Rhône, Loire and Germany stand out, with top producers galore. Then there are Loeb's new discoveries from Spain and the New World, especially New Zealand and South Africa.*

Maison du Vin

Moor Hill, Hawkhurst, Kent TN18 4PF (01580) 753487
fax (01580) 755627 e-mail kvgriffin@aol.com website www.maison-du-vin.co.uk hours Mon 10–4, Tue and Thu
10–8, Wed and Fri 10–5, Sat 10–6 cards Access, AmEx, Maestro, MasterCard, Visa delivery Free locally; UK mainland
at cost en primeur Bordeaux. C G M T
✪ *As the name suggests, the focus is on French wines, at prices from about £6 upwards. There's a monthly themed 'wine school' or you can book personal tutored tastings.*

Majestic

(see also Wine and Beer World page 109)

head office Majestic House, Otterspool Way, Watford, Herts WD25 8WW (01923) 298200
fax (01923) 819105; 136 stores nationwide e-mail info@majestic.co.uk website www.majestic.co.uk
hours Mon–Fri 10–8, Sat 9–7, Sun 10–5 (may vary) cards AmEx, Diners, Maestro, MasterCard, Visa
delivery Free UK mainland minimum order 1 mixed case (12 bottles) en primeur Bordeaux, Port, Burgundy. G M T
© *One of the best places to buy Champagne, with a good range and good discounts for buying in quantity. Loads of interesting and reasonably priced stuff, especially from France and the New World.*

Marks & Spencer

head office Waterside House, 35 North Wharf Road, London W2 1NW (020) 7935 4422
fax (020) 7487 2679; 500 licensed stores website www.marksandspencer.com hours Variable
discounts Variable, Wine of the Month, buy any 6 and save 10% in selected stores. M T
© *M&S works with top producers around the world to create its impressive list of own-label wines.*

Martinez Wines

35 The Grove, Ilkley, Leeds, West Yorkshire LS29 9NJ (01943) 600000
fax 0870 922 3940 e-mail julian@martinez.co.uk website www.martinez.co.uk
hours Sun 12–6, Mon–Wed 10–8, Thurs–Fri 10–9, Sat 9.30–6 cards AmEx, Maestro, MasterCard, Visa
discounts 5% on 6 bottles or more, 10% off orders over £150 delivery Free local delivery, otherwise £11 per case mainland UK en primeur Bordeaux, Burgundy. C G M T
© *Carefully chosen selection – Alsace and Beaujolais look spot-on, as do Bordeaux, Burgundy and Rhône, so I would trust their selection from other regions.*

Millésima

87 Quai de Paludate, BP 89, 33038 Bordeaux Cedex, France (00 33) 5 57 80 88 08
fax (00 33) 5 57 80 88 19 Freephone 0800 917 0352 website www.millesima.com hours Mon–Fri 8–5.30
cards AmEx, Diners, Maestro, MasterCard, Visa delivery For bottled wines, free to single UK addresses for orders exceeding £500. Otherwise, a charge of £20 will be applied. For en primeur wines, free to single UK addresses.
en primeur Bordeaux, Burgundy, Rhône. C M T
© *Wine comes direct from the châteaux to Millésima's cellars, where 3 million bottles are stored. A sprinkling of established names from other French regions.*

Montrachet

mail order 59 Kennington Road, London SE1 7PZ (020) 7928 1990

fax (020) 7928 3415   e-mail andy@montrachetwine.com   website www.montrachetwine.com

hours (Office and mail order) Mon–Fri 8.30–5.30   cards Maestro, MasterCard, Visa   delivery England and Wales £12 including VAT, free for 3 or more cases; for Scotland ring for details   minimum order 1 unmixed case en primeur Bordeaux, Burgundy.   M T

✪ *Impressive Burgundies are the main attraction here, but there are also some very good Rhônes, and Bordeaux is excellent at all price levels.*

Moreno Wines

11 Marylands Road, London W9 2DU (020) 7286 0678

fax (020) 7286 0513   e-mail merchant@moreno-wines.co.uk   website www.morenowinedirect.com

hours Mon–Fri 4–9, Sat 12–9   cards AmEx, Maestro, MasterCard, Visa   discounts 10% 2 or more cases delivery Free locally, 3 or more cases within UK also free, otherwise £7.50.   M T

✪ *Specialist in Spanish wines, some fine and rare, with prices to match, but plenty of everyday drinking too, including whites and rosados.*

Moriarty Vintners

Unit 3, Penarth Road Retail Park, Penarth Road, Cardiff CF11 8TW (02920) 705572

fax (02920) 488300   e-mail david@moriarty-vintners.co.uk   website www.moriarty-vintners.co.uk

hours Mon–Thurs 10–6, Fri–Sat 10–8, Sun 12–5   discounts 15% off mixed case   delivery free locally, nationwide at cost   en primeur Italy, Port, Rhône.   C G M T

✪ *Concentrates on exciting gems from small producers. Italy is strong and other regions with good coverage include the Languedoc, Bordeaux, Australia and Spain.*

Wm Morrison Supermarkets

head office Hilmore House, Gain Lane, Bradford, West Yorkshire BD3 7DL 0845 611 5000

fax 0845 611 6801   customer service 0845 611 6111; 371 licensed branches   website www.morrisons.co.uk

hours Variable, generally Mon–Sat 8–8, Sun 10–4   cards Amex, Delta, Maestro, MasterCard, Solo, Style, Visa Electron.   G T

✪ *Inexpensive, often tasty wines, and if you're prepared to trade up a little there's some really good stuff here.*

The following services are available where indicated: **C** = cellarage **G** = glass hire/loan **M** = mail/online order **T** = tastings and talks

James Nicholson

7/9 Killyleagh Street, Crossgar, Co. Down, Northern Ireland BT30 9DQ (028) 4483 0091
fax (028) 4483 0028 e-mail shop@jnwine.com website www.jnwine.com hours Mon–Sat 10–7
cards Maestro, MasterCard, Visa discounts 10% mixed case delivery Free (1 case or more) in Eire and Northern
Ireland; UK mainland £10.95, 2 cases £5.95 en primeur Bordeaux, Burgundy, California, Rioja, Rhône. C G M T
☺ *Well-chosen list mainly from small, committed growers around the world. Bordeaux, Rhône and southern France are*
slightly ahead of the field, there's a good selection of Burgundy and some excellent drinking from Germany and Spain.

Nickolls & Perks

37 Lower High Street, Stourbridge, West Midlands DY8 1TA (01384) 394518
fax (01384) 440786 e-mail sales@nickollsandperks.co.uk website www.nickollsandperks.co.uk
hours Tues–Fri 10.30–5.30, Sat 10.30–5 cards Maestro, MasterCard, Visa discounts negotiable per case
delivery £10 per consignment en primeur Bordeaux, Champagne, Port. C G M T
☺ *Established in 1797, Nickolls & Perks have a wide-ranging list – and a terrific website – covering most areas.*
Their strength is France. Advice is available to clients wishing to develop their cellars or invest in wine.

Nidderdale Fine Wines

2a High Street, Pateley Bridge, North Yorkshire HG3 5AW (01423) 711703
e-mail info@southaustralianwines.com website www.southaustralianwines.com hours Tues–Sat 10–6, Sun 12–5
cards Maestro, MasterCard, Visa discounts 5% case discount on shop purchases delivery £5 per case in England,
Wales and southern Scotland. Single bottle delivery available. G T
☺ *Specialist in South Australia, with 300 wines broken down into regions. Also 350 or so wines from other parts*
of Australia and the rest of the world. Look out for online offers and winemaker dinners.

Noble Rot Wine Warehouses

18 Market Street, Bromsgrove, Worcestershire, B61 8JZ (01527) 575606 fax (01527) 833133
e-mail info@noble-rot.co.uk website www.noble-rot.co.uk hours Mon–Fri 10–7, Sat 9.30–6.30
cards Maestro, MasterCard, Visa discounts Various delivery Free within 10-mile radius. G T
☺ *Great for current drinking, mostly at £4 to £15 a bottle. Australia, Italy, France and Spain feature strongly*
in a frequently changing list of more than 400 wines.

The Nobody Inn

Doddiscombsleigh, Nr Exeter, Devon EX6 7PS (01647) 252394
fax (01647) 252978 e-mail info@nobodyinn.co.uk website www.nobodyinn.co.uk
hours Mon–Sun 12–3 & 6–11 (summer) cards AmEx, Maestro, MasterCard, Visa
discounts 5% per case delivery £7.99 for 1 case, free over £150. G M T
• The Nobody Wine Company (01647) 252394 fax (01647) 252978 e-mail sales@thenobodywinecompany.co.uk
website www.thenobodywinecompany.co.uk hours 24-hr ordering service delivery Free for orders over £150.
✪ *The 16th-century Nobody Inn has an extraordinary list of more than 700 wines. Australia rules, but there's something exciting from just about everywhere, including marvellous sweet wines. The Wine Company is a mail-order venture for wines mostly priced at £5–10.*

Oddbins

head office 31–33 Weir Road, London SW19 8UG (020) 8944 4400
fax (020) 8944 4411 mail order Oddbins Direct 0800 328 2323 fax 0800 328 3848; 173 shops nationwide
website www.oddbins.com hours Ask local branch for details cards AmEx, Maestro, MasterCard, Visa
discounts 6 for 5 on Champagne or sparkling wine; 10% off 6 bottles or 20% off 12 bottles of table wine, excluding fine wine; regular general promotions delivery (Stores) free locally for orders over £100 en primeur Bordeaux. G M T
• Calais store Cité Europe, 139 Rue de Douvres, 62901, Coquelles Cedex, France (0033) 3 21 82 07 32
fax (0033) 3 21 82 05 83 pre-order www.oddbins.com/storefinder/calais.asp
✪ *New World meets the classic regions of Europe: extensive Aussie selection, well-chosen Chileans, Argentinians and South Africans sit alongside good stuff from all over France, Spain and Italy. Always a good choice of fizz.*

The Oxford Wine Company

The Wine Warehouse, Witney Road, Standlake, Oxon OX29 7PR (01865) 301144
fax (01865) 301155 e-mail info@oxfordwine.co.uk website www.oxfordwine.co.uk
hours Mon–Sat 9–7, Sun 11–4 cards AmEx, Diners, Maestro, MasterCard, Visa discounts 5% discount on a case of 12, no minimum order delivery Free locally; national delivery £9.99 for any amount en primeur Bordeaux. G M T
✪ *A good selection from the classic regions and the New World, from bargain basement prices to expensive fine wines. Easy-to-use website. They also organize tastings and other events.*

OZ WINES

mail order Freepost Lon 17656, London SW18 5BR, 0845 450 1261
fax (020) 8870 8839 e-mail sales@ozwines.co.uk website www.ozwines.co.uk hours Mon–Fri 9.30–7
cards Access, Diners, Maestro, MasterCard, Visa delivery Free minimum order 1 mixed case. M T
✪ *Australian wines made by small wineries and real people – wines with the kind of thrilling flavours that Australians do better than anyone else.*

Penistone Court Wine Cellars

The Railway Station, Penistone, Sheffield, South Yorkshire S36 6HP (01226) 766037
fax (01226) 767310 e-mail chris@pcwine.plus.com website www.pcwine.co.uk hours Tues–Fri 10–6, Sat 10–3
cards Maestro, MasterCard, Visa delivery Free locally, rest of UK mainland charged at cost 1 case or more
minimum order 1 case. G M
✪ *A well-balanced list, with something from just about everywhere, mostly from familiar names.*

Philglas & Swiggot

21 Northcote Road, Battersea, London SW11 1NG (020) 7924 4494
• 64 Hill Rise, Richmond, London TW10 6UB (020) 8332 6031
• 22 New Quebec Street, Marylebone, London W1H 7SB (020) 7402 0002
e-mail info@philglas-swiggot.co.uk website www.philglas-swiggot.co.uk hours (Battersea and Richmond) Mon–Sat
11–7, Sun 12–5; (Marylebone) Mon–Sat 11–7 cards AmEx, Maestro, MasterCard, Visa discounts 5% per case
delivery Free 1 case locally. G M
✪ *Excellent selections from Australia, Italy, France and Austria – subtle, interesting wines, not blockbuster brands.*

Christopher Piper Wines

1 Silver Street, Ottery St Mary, Devon EX11 1DB (01404) 814139
fax (01404) 812100 e-mail sales@christopherpiperwines.co.uk website www.christopherpiperwines.co.uk
hours Mon–Fri 8.30–5.30, Sat 9–4.30 cards Maestro, MasterCard, Visa discounts 5% mixed case, 10% 3 or more
cases delivery Free for orders over £190, otherwise £7.05 per case minimum order (for mail order) 1 mixed case
en primeur Bordeaux, Burgundy, Rhône. C G M T
✪ *Huge range of well-chosen wines that reflect a sense of place and personality, with lots of information to help you make up your mind.*

Terry Platt Wine Merchants

Council Street West, Llandudno LL30 1ED (01492) 874099

fax (01492) 874788 e-mail info@terryplattwines.co.uk website www.terryplattwines.co.uk

hours Mon–Fri 8.30–5.30 cards Access, Maestro, MasterCard, Visa delivery Free locally and UK mainland 5 cases or more minimum order 1 mixed case. G M T

○ *A wide-ranging list with a sprinkling of good growers from most regions. New World coverage has increased recently.*

Playford Ros

Middle Park, Thirsk, Yorkshire YO7 3AH (01845) 526777

fax (01845) 526888 e-mail sales@playfordros.com website www.playfordros.com

hours Mon–Fri 8–6 cards MasterCard, Visa discounts negotiable delivery Free Yorkshire, Derbyshire, Durham, Newcastle; elsewhere £10–15 or at courier cost minimum order 1 mixed case en primeur Bordeaux, Burgundy. G M T

○ *A carefully chosen list, with reassuringly recognizable Burgundy, exceptional Australian and good stuff from other French regions, Chile, Oregon and New Zealand. Plenty at the £6–8 mark.*

Portland Wine Co

16 North Parade, off Norris Road, Sale, Cheshire M33 3JS (0161) 962 8752

fax (0161) 905 1291 • 152a Ashley Road, Hale WA15 9SA (0161) 928 0357 • 82 Chester Road, Macclesfield SK11 8DL (01625) 616147 e-mail enquiries@portlandwine.co.uk website www.portlandwine.co.uk

hours Mon–Sat 10–10, Sun 12–9.30 cards Maestro, MasterCard, Visa discounts 5% 2 cases or more, 10% 5 cases or more delivery Free locally, £15 + VAT per consignment nationwide, no minimum order en primeur Bordeaux. C T

○ *Spain, Portugal and Burgundy are specialities and there's a promising-looking list of clarets. Consumer-friendly list with something at every price level from around the world.*

Quaff Fine Wine Merchant

139–141 Portland Road, Hove BN3 5QJ (01273) 820320

fax (01273) 820326 e-mail sales@quaffit.com website www.quaffit.com hours Mon–Thurs 10–7, Fri–Sat 10–8, Sun 12–7 cards Access, Maestro, MasterCard, Visa discounts 10% mixed case delivery Next working day nationwide, charge depends on order value. C G M T

○ *Extensive and keenly-priced list organized by grape variety rather than country.*

Raeburn Fine Wines

21–23 Comely Bank Road, Edinburgh EH4 1DS (0131) 343 1159
fax (0131) 332 5166 e-mail sales@raeburnfinewines.com website www.raeburnfinewines.com
hours Mon–Sat 9.30–6 cards AmEx, Maestro, MasterCard, Visa discounts 5% unsplit case, 2.5% mixed
delivery Free local area 1 or more cases (usually); elsewhere at cost en primeur Australia, Bordeaux, Burgundy, California, Germany, Italy, Languedoc-Roussillon, Loire, New Zealand, Rhône. G M T
○ *Carefully-chosen list, mainly from small growers. Burgundy and Loire are specialities, with Italy, Austria and northern Spain close behind.*

Real Wine Co.

1 Cannon Meadow, Bull Lane, Gerrards Cross, Buckinghamshire SL9 8RE (01753) 885619
e-mail mark@therealwineco.co.uk website www.therealwineco.co.uk cards Delta, Maestro, Mastercard, Visa
delivery Up to 2 cases £5, free for 3 or more cases to single address; free to postcodes SL9 and HP9 irrespective of number of cases minimum order 1 mixed case
○ *Owner Mark Hughes has based his list entirely on his personal taste – check it out and see if you agree with his lively tasting notes. There are plenty of good-value wines, including several rosés.*

Reid Wines

The Mill, Marsh Lane, Hallatrow, Nr Bristol BS39 6EB (01761) 452645 fax (01761) 453642 e-mail reidwines@aol.com
hours Mon–Fri 9–5.30 cards Access, Maestro, MasterCard, Visa (3% charge) delivery Free within 25 miles of Hallatrow (Bristol), and in central London for orders over 2 cases en primeur Claret. C G M T
○ *A mix of great old wines, some old duds and splendid current stuff. Italy, USA, Australia, port and Madeira look tremendous.*

Richardson & Sons

26a Lowther Street, Whitehaven, Cumbria CA28 7DG
fax/tel (01946) 65334 e-mail mailwines@tiscali.co.uk hours Mon–Sat 10–5.30 cards AmEx, Delta, Maestro, MasterCard, Visa delivery Free locally. M T
○ *Focused on reds from Australia, Bordeaux and Burgundy, with a preference for small producers. Join their mailing list to get regular updates.*

Howard Ripley

25 Dingwall Road, London SW18 3AZ (020) 8877 3065

fax (020) 8877 0029 e-mail info@howardripley.com website www.howardripley.com
hours Mon–Fri 9–6, Sat 9–1 cards Maestro, MasterCard, Visa delivery Minimum charge £10.50 + VAT, free UK
mainland on orders over £500 ex-VAT minimum order 1 case en primeur Burgundy, Germany. C M T
✪ *A must-have list for serious Burgundy lovers; expensive but not excessive. The German range is also excellent.*

Roberson

348 Kensington High Street, London W14 8NS (020) 7371 2121

fax (020) 7371 4010 e-mail retail@roberson.co.uk website www.robersonwinemerchant.co.uk, www.roberson.co.uk
hours Mon–Sat 10–8, Sun 12–6 cards Access, AmEx, Maestro, MasterCard, Visa discounts mail order 5% on
champagne and spirits, 10% or wine cases delivery Free delivery within London, otherwise £15 per case
en primeur Bordeaux, Port. C G M T
✪ *Fine and rare wines, sold by the bottle. All of France is excellent; so is Italy and port.*

The RSJ Wine Company

33 Coin Street, London SE1 9NR (020) 7928 4554

fax (020) 7928 9768 e-mail tom.king@rsj.uk.com website www.rsj.uk.com
hours Mon–Fri 9–6, answering machine at other times cards AmEx, Maestro, MasterCard, Visa delivery Free central
London, minimum 1 case; England and Wales (per case), £14.10 1 case, £10.25 2 cases or more. G M T
✪ *A roll-call of great Loire names, and some good Bordeaux.*

Sainsbury's

head office 33 Holborn, London EC1N 2HT (020) 7695 6000
customer service 0800 636262; 800 stores website www. sainsburys.co.uk – click on Wines by the case for exciting
and exclusive offers hours Variable, some 24 hrs, locals generally Mon–Sat 7–11, Sun 10 or 11–4
cards AmEx, Maestro, MasterCard, Visa discounts 5% for 6 bottles or more G M T
● mail order 0800 917 4092 fax 0800 917 4095
● Calais store Sainsbury's, Centre Commercial Auchan, Route de Boulogne, 62100 Calais, France (0033) 3 21 82 38 48
preorder www.sainsburys.co.uk and click on Wine at Calais
✪ *A collection to cater for bargain hunters as well as lovers of good-value wine higher up the scale. They've expanded their
Taste the difference range and got some top producers on board.*

Savage Selection

The Ox House, Market Place, Northleach, Cheltenham, Glos GL54 3EG (01451) 860896
fax (01451) 860996 • The Ox House Shop and Wine Bar at same address (01451) 860680
e-mail wine@savageselection.co.uk website www.savageselection.co.uk hours Office: Mon–Fri 9–6; shop: Tue–Wed
10–7.30, Thur–Fri 10–10, Sat 10–4 cards Maestro, MasterCard, Visa delivery Free locally for orders over £100;
elsewhere on UK mainland free for orders over £250: otherwise £11.75 per consignment en primeur Bordeaux. C G M T
☺ *Owner Mark Savage seeks out new and interesting wines from Italy, Spain, Germany and Austria, as well as from
Hungary, Greece, Slovenia and Oregon.*

Seckford Wines

Dock Lane, Melton, Suffolk IP12 1PE (01394) 446622
fax (01394) 446633 e-mail sales@seckfordwines.co.uk website www.seckfordwines.co.uk
cards Maestro, MasterCard, Visa delivery £11.75 inc VAT per consignment, UK mainland; elsewhere at cost
minimum order 1 mixed case en primeur Bordeaux, Burgundy. C M
☺ *Bordeaux, Burgundy, Champagne and the Rhône are the stars of this list, with some excellent older vintages. Serious
stuff from Italy and Spain, too.*

Selfridges

400 Oxford Street, London W1A 1AB 0800 123 400 (for all stores) fax (020) 7318 3768
• Upper Mall East, Bullring, Birmingham B5 4BP
• 1 Exchange Square, Manchester M3 1BD
• The Trafford Centre, Manchester M17 8DA
fax (01394) 446633 e-mail wineshop@selfridges.co.uk website www.selfridges.com hours London Mon–Sat 9.30–8
(Thurs –9pm), Sun 11.30–6.15; Birmingham Mon–Sat 10–8 (Thurs –9), Sun 10.30–5; Manchester Exchange Mon–Fri
10–8 (Thurs –9), Sat 9–8, Sun 10.30–5; Manchester Trafford Mon–Sat 10–10 (Thurs –9), Sun 12–6; cards Maestro,
MasterCard, Visa discounts 10% case discount delivery variable T
☺ *Strong fine wine list. Great selection for gifts and regular tastings. Also strong on spirits.*

The following services are available where indicated: **C** = cellarage **G** = glass hire/loan **M** = mail/online order **T** = tastings and talks

Somerfield

head office Somerfield House, Whitchurch Lane, Bristol BS14 0TJ (0117) 935 9359
fax (0117) 935 6669; 940 Somerfield stores website www.somerfield.co.uk
hours Mon–Sat 8–8, Sun 10–4 cards Maestro, MasterCard, Visa discounts 5% off 6 bottles
delivery Free local delivery for orders over £25 in selected stores.

○ *Wines from all over, ranging from bargain prices to the £25 mark. Lots of choice on New World wines, including award-winning Pinot Grigio from Chile and Syrah rosé from Chile.*

Sommelier Wine Co.

23 St George's Esplanade, St Peter Port, Guernsey, Channel Islands, GY1 2BG (01481) 721677
fax (01481) 716818 hours Mon–Sat 9.15–5.30, except Fri 9.15–6 cards Maestro, MasterCard, Visa
discounts 5% 1 case or more delivery Free locally 1 mixed case. Customs legislation means that the shipping of wine
to the UK mainland is restricted. G T

○ *An excellent list, with interesting, unusual wines. A big selection of top-notch Australia, Italy, Loire, Beaujolais, Burgundy, Bordeaux, the Rhône, Spain and South Africa.*

Frank Stainton Wines

1 Station Yard, Station Road, Kendal, Cumbria LA9 6BT (01539) 731886 fax (01539) 730396
e-mail admin@stainton-wines.co.uk website www.stainton-wines.co.uk hours Mon–Fri 9–5.30, Sat 9–4.30
cards Maestro, MasterCard, Visa discounts 5% mixed case delivery Free Cumbria and North Lancashire;
elsewhere (per case) £13 1 case, more than 1 case variable. G M T

○ *The list includes some great Bordeaux, interesting Burgundy, and leading names from Italy and Chile.*

Stevens Garnier

47 West Way, Botley, Oxford OX2 0JF (01865) 263303
fax (01865) 791594 e-mail shop@stevensgarnier.co.uk hours Mon–Thur 10–6, Fri 10–7, Sat 9.30–5.30
cards AmEx, Maestro, MasterCard, Visa, Solo discounts 5% on a mixed case delivery Free locally; 'competitive rates'
elsewhere. G M T

○ *Regional France is a strength: this is one of the few places in the UK you can buy wine from Savoie. Likewise, there are interesting choices from Portugal, Australia, Chile and Canada.*

Stone, Vine & Sun

No. 13 Humphrey Farms, Hazeley Road, Twyford, Winchester SO21 1QA (01962) 712351
fax (01962) 717545 e-mail sales@stonevine.co.uk website www.stonevine.co.uk
hours Mon–Fri 9–6, Sat 9.30–4 cards Access, Maestro, MasterCard, Visa discounts 5% on an unmixed case
delivery £5 for 1st case, £8.50 for 2 cases, free for orders over £250. Prices vary for Scottish Highlands, islands
and Northern Ireland. G M T
☼ *Lovely list marked by enthusiasm and passion for the subject. Lots of interesting stuff from France, but also from
Germany, South Africa, New Zealand and elsewhere.*

Sunday Times Wine Club

New Aquitaine House, Exeter Way, Theale, Reading, Berks RG7 4PL
order line 0870 220 0020 fax 0870 220 0030 e-mail orders@sundaytimeswineclub.co.uk
website www.sundaytimeswineclub.co.uk hours Mon–Fri 8–11, Sat–Sun 8–9
cards AmEx, Diners, Maestro, MasterCard, Visa delivery £5.99 per order en primeur Australia, Bordeaux, Burgundy,
Rhône. C M T
☼ *Essentially the same as Laithwaites (see page 92), though the special offers come round at different times.
The membership fee is £10 per annum. The club runs tours and tasting events for its members.*

T & W Wines

5 Station Way, Brandon, Suffolk IP27 0BH (01842) 814414
fax (01842) 819967 e-mail contact@tw-wines.com website www.tw-wines.com hours Mon–Fri 9.30–5.30,
occasional Sat 9.30–1 cards AmEx, MasterCard, Visa delivery (Most areas) 7–23 bottles £15.95 + VAT, 2 or more
cases free en primeur Burgundy. C G M T
☼ *A good list, particularly if you're looking for Burgundy, Rhône, Alsace or the Loire, but prices are not especially low.*

Tanners

26 Wyle Cop, Shrewsbury, Shropshire SY1 1XD (01743) 234500 fax (01743) 234501
• 4 St Peter's Square, Hereford HR1 2PG (01432) 272044 fax (01432) 263316
• 36 High Street, Bridgnorth WV16 4DB (01746) 763148 fax (01746) 769798
• Severn Farm Enterprise Park, Welshpool SY21 7DF (01938) 552542 fax (01938) 556565
e-mail sales@tanners-wines.co.uk website www.tanners-wines.co.uk hours Shrewsbury Mon–Sat 9–6, branches
9–5.30 cards AmEx, Maestro, MasterCard, Visa discounts 5% 1 mixed case, 7.5% 5 mixed cases (cash & collection);

5% for 3 mixed cases, 7.5% for 5 (mail order) mail order delivery Free 1 mixed case over £90, otherwise £7.50 minimum order £25 en primeur Bordeaux, Burgundy, Rhône, Germany, Port. C G M T

✪ *Outstanding, award-winning merchant: Bordeaux, Burgundy and Germany are terrific.*

Tesco
head office Tesco House, PO Box 18, Delamare Road, Cheshunt EN8 9SL (01992) 632222
fax (01992) 630794 customer service 0800 505555; 916 licensed branches e-mail customer.services@tesco.co.uk
website www.tesco.com hours Variable cards Maestro, MasterCard, Visa discount 5% on 6 bottles or more G M T
• Calais store Tesco Vin Plus, Cité Europe, 122 Boulevard du Kent, 62231 Coquelles, France (0033) 3 21 46 02 70
website www.tesco.com/vinplus; www.tesco-france.com hours Mon–Sat 8.30–10pm

✪ *Premium wines at around £20 down to bargain basement bottles. Tesco.com has an even greater selection by the case.*

Thresher Group: Thresher Wine Shops and Wine Rack
head office Enjoyment Hall, Bessemer Road, Welwyn Garden City, Herts AL7 1BL (01707) 387200
fax (01707) 387350 website www.threshergroup.com; 840 Thresher Wine Shops, 266 Wine Rack stores
hours Mon–Sat 10–10 (some 10.30), Sun 11–10, Scotland 12.30–10.30 cards Maestro, MasterCard, Visa
delivery Free locally, some branches. G T

✪ *Australia and France take the leading roles, with strong support from Spain, New Zealand and South Africa. The popular 3 for 2 deal means you'll get some real bargains if you buy any 3 bottles – but some single bottle prices are on the high side.*

Turville Valley Wines
The Firs, Potter Row, Great Missenden, Bucks HP16 9LT (01494) 868818
fax (01494) 868832 e-mail chris@turville-valley-wines.com website www.turville-valley-wines.com
hours Mon–Fri 9–5.30 cards None delivery By arrangement minimum order £300/12 bottles. C M

✪ *Serious wines for serious spenders.*

Valvona & Crolla
19 Elm Row, Edinburgh EH7 4AA (0131) 556 6066 fax (0131) 556 1668
e-mail wine@valvonacrolla.co.uk website www.valvonacrolla.com hours Shop: Mon–Sat 8–6.30, Sun 10.30–5, Caffe
bar: Mon–Sat 8–6, Sun 10.30–4.30 cards AmEx, Maestro, MasterCard, Visa discounts 7% 1–3 cases, 10% 4 or more
delivery Free on orders over £150, otherwise £9; Saturdays free on orders over £200, otherwise £15. G M T

✪ *A fabulous selection of wines from every region of Italy, including Sicily and Sardinia.*

Villeneuve Wines

1 Venlaw Court, Peebles, Scotland EH45 8AE (01721) 722500 fax (01721) 729922

• 82 High Street, Haddington EH41 3ET (01620) 822224

• 49A Broughton Street, Edinburgh EH1 3RJ (0131) 558 8441

e-mail wines@villeneuvewines.com website www.villeneuvewines.com hours (Peebles) Mon–Sat 9–8, Sun 12.30–5.30; (Haddington) Mon–Sat 9–7; (Edinburgh) Mon–Wed 12.30–10, Thurs 10–10, Fri–Sat 9–10, Sun 12.30–10 cards AmEx, Maestro, MasterCard, Visa discounts 5% per case delivery Free locally, £8.50 per case elsewhere. G M T
○ Italy, California, Australia and New Zealand are all marvellous here. Spain is clearly an enthusiasm, too.

Vinceremos

Munro House, Duke Street, Leeds LS9 8AG 0800 107 3086 fax (0113) 288 4566

e-mail info@vinceremos.co.uk website www.vinceremos.co.uk hours Mon–Fri 8.30–5.30 cards AmEx, Delta, Maestro, MasterCard, Visa discounts 5% on 5 cases or over, 10% on 10 cases or over delivery Free 5 cases or more M
○ Organic specialist, with a wide-ranging list of wines, including biodynamic and Fairtrade.

Vin du Van Wine Merchants

mail order Colthups, The Street, Appledore, Kent TN26 2BX (01233) 758727 fax (01233) 758389 hours Mon–Fri 9–5 cards Delta, Maestro, MasterCard, Visa delivery Free locally; elsewhere £5.95 for first case, further cases free. Highlands and islands, ask for quote minimum order 1 mixed case. M
○ Extensive, wonderfully quirky, star-studded Australian list, the kind of inspired lunacy I'd take with me to read on a desert island.

Vintage Roots

Farley Farms, Reading Road, Arborfield, Berkshire, RG2 9HT (0118) 976 1999 fax (0118) 976 1998 hours Mon–Fri 8.30–5.30, Saturdays in December e-mail info@vintageroots.co.uk website www.vintageroots.co.uk cards Delta, Maestro, MasterCard, Visa discounts 5% on 5 cases or over delivery £6.95 for any delivery under 5 cases; more than 6 cases is free. Some local deliveries free. Cases can be mixed. Overnight is an extra £2.50 per case. G M T
○ Everything on this list is organic and/or biodynamic, from Champagne and other fizz to beer and cider.

The following services are available where indicated: **C** = cellarage **G** = glass hire/loan **M** = mail/online order **T** = tastings and talks

Virgin Wines

mail order The Loft, St James' Mill, Whitefriars, Norwich NR3 1TN 0870 164 9593
fax (01603) 619277 e-mail help@virginwines.com website www.virginwines.com
hours (Office) Mon–Fri 8.30–6.30, Sat 10–4, Internet 24 hrs cards AmEx, Maestro, MasterCard, Visa
discounts Regular special offers delivery £5.99 per order for all UK deliveries minimum order 1 case. M T
✪ *Online retailer with reasonably priced wines from all over the world. Well-balanced pre-mixed cases, or you can mix your own.*

Waitrose

head office Doncastle Road, Southern Industrial Area, Bracknell, Berkshire RG12 8YA
customer service 0800 188884, 185 licensed stores e-mail customerservice@waitrose.co.uk
website www.waitrose.com/wine hours Mon–Sat 8.30–7, 8 or 9, Sun 10–4 or 11–5
cards AmEx, Delta, Maestro, MasterCard, Partnership Card, Visa
discounts Regular monthly promotions, 5% off for 6 bottles or more
home delivery Available through www.waitrosedeliver.co.uk and www.ocado.com and Waitrose Wine Direct (below)
en primeur Bordeaux and Burgundy available through Waitrose Wine Direct G T
• waitrose wine direct order online at www.waitrose.com/wine or 0800 188881
e-mail wineadvisor@johnlewis.com discounts Vary monthly on featured cases; branch promotions are matched. All cases include a 5% discount to match branch offer.
delivery Free standard delivery throughout UK mainland, Northern Ireland and Isle of Wight. Named day delivery – £6.95 per addressee (order by 3pm for next working day). Now includes Sat. Next day delivery pre-10.30am – £9.95 per addressee (order by 3pm for next working day).
✪ *Ahead of the other supermarkets in quality, value and imagination. Still lots of tasty stuff under £5.*

Waterloo Wine Co

office and warehouse 6 Vine Yard, London SE1 1QL
shop 59–61 Lant Street, London SE1 1QL (020) 7403 7967 fax (020) 7357 6976 e-mail sales@waterloowine.co.uk
website www.waterloowine.co.uk hours Mon–Fri 11–7.30, Sat 10–5
cards AmEx, Maestro, MasterCard, Visa
delivery Free 5 cases in central London (otherwise £5); elsewhere, 1 case £12, 2 cases £7.50 each. G T
✪ *Quirky, personal list, strong in the Loire and New Zealand.*

Whitesides of Clitheroe

Shawbridge Street, Clitheroe, Lancs BB7 1NA (01200) 422281 fax (01200) 427129
e-mail whitesides.wine@btconnect.com hours Mon–Fri 9–5.30, Sat 10–4
cards Maestro, MasterCard, Visa
discounts 5% per case delivery Free locally, elsewhere at cost. G M T
✪ *Half New World, half Europe, with some interesting selections hidden among the sub-£5 stuff.*

Wimbledon Wine Cellar

1 Gladstone Road, Wimbledon, London SW19 1QU (020) 8540 9979 fax (020) 8540 9399
• 84 Chiswick High Road, London W4 1SY (020) 8994 7989 fax (020) 8994 3683
• 4 The Boulevard, Imperial Wharf, Chelsea, London SW6 2UB (020) 7736 2191
e-mail enquiries@ wimbledonwinecellar.com, chiswick@wimbledonwinecellar.com or chelsea@wimbledonwinecellar.com
website www.wimbledonwinecellar.com hours Mon–Sat 10–9, Sun 11–7 (all stores)
cards AmEx, Maestro, MasterCard, Visa discounts 10% off 1 case (with a few exceptions), 20% off case of Champagne
delivery Free local delivery. Courier charges elsewhere en primeur Burgundy, Bordeaux, Tuscany, Rhône. C G M T
✪ *Top names from Italy, Burgundy, Bordeaux, Rhône, Loire – and some of the best of the New World.*

Wine & Beer World (Majestic)

head office Majestic House, Otterspool Way, Watford, Herts WD25 8WW (01923) 298200
fax (01923) 819105 e-mail info@wineandbeer.co.uk website www.wineandbeer.co.uk
• Rue du Judée, Zone Marcel Doret, Calais 62100, France (0033) 3 21 97 63 00
• Centre Commercial Carrefour, Quai L'Entrepôt, Cherbourg 50100, France (0033) 2 33 22 23 22
• Unit 3A, Zone La Française, Coquelles 62331, France (0033) 3 21 82 93 64
pre-order (01923) 298297 hours (Calais) 7 days 8–10; (Cherbourg) Mon–Sat 9–7.30; (Coquelles) 7 days 8–8. Calais
and Coquelles open Bank Holidays at the usual times. Free ferry crossing from Dover to Calais when your pre-order
is over £300. cards Maestro, MasterCard, Visa. T
✪ *The French arm of Majestic, with savings of up to 50% on UK prices. Calais is the largest branch and Coquelles
the nearest to the Channel Tunnel terminal. English-speaking staff.*

Winemark

3 Duncrue Place, Belfast BT3 9BU (028) 9074 6274 fax (028) 9074 8022; 71 branches e-mail info@ winemark.com
website www.winemark.com hours Branches vary, but in general Mon–Sat 10–10, Sun 12–8

cards Delta, Maestro, MasterCard, Visa discounts 5% on 6–11 bottles, 10% on 12 bottles or more. G M T
☼ *Strong in the New World, with some interesting Australia, New Zealand, Chile and California.*

Wine Rack
See Thresher Group.

The Wine Society
Gunnels Wood Road, Stevenage, Herts SG1 2BG (01438) 741177 fax (01438) 761167 order line (01438) 740222
e-mail memberservices@thewinesociety.com website www.thewinesociety.com
hours Mon–Fri 8.30–9, Sat 9–5; showroom: Mon–Fri 10–6, Thurs 10–7, Sat 9.30–5.30
cards Maestro, MasterCard, Visa discounts (per case) £3 per collection delivery Free 1 case or more UK mainland and
Northern Ireland. Collection facility at Montreuil, France, at French rates of duty and VAT
en primeur Bordeaux, Burgundy, Germany, Port, Rhône.
☼ *An outstanding list from an inspired wine-buying team. Masses of well-chosen affordable wines as well as big names.*

Wine Treasury
mail order 69–71 Bondway, London SW8 1SQ (020) 7793 9999
fax (020) 7793 8080 e-mail bottled@winetreasury.com website www.winetreasury.com hours Mon–Fri 9.30–6
cards Maestro, MasterCard, Visa discounts 10% for unmixed dozens delivery Free for orders over £200, England and
Wales; Scotland phone for more details minimum order 1 mixed case. M T
☼ *Excellent choices and top names from California and Italy – but they don't come cheap.*

The Winery
4 Clifton Road, London W9 1SS (020) 7286 6475 fax (020) 7286 2733 e-mail info@thewineryuk.com
website www.thewineryuk.com hours Mon–Sat 11–9.30, Sun and public holidays 12–8 cards Maestro, MasterCard,
Visa discounts 5% on a mixed case delivery Free locally or for 3 cases or more, otherwise £10 per case. G M T
☼ *Largest selection of dry German wines in the UK. Burgundy, Rhône, Champagne, Italy and California are other specialities.*

Wines of Westhorpe
136a Doncaster Road, Mexborough, South Yorkshire S64 0JW (01709) 584863 fax (01709) 584863
e-mail wines@westhorpe.co.uk website www. westhorpe.co.uk hours Mon–Thu 9–8, Fri–Sat 9–6

cards Maestro, MasterCard, Visa discounts Variable on 2 dozen or more delivery Free UK mainland (except northern Scotland) minimum order 1 mixed case. M

☼ *An excellent list for devotees of Eastern European wines – especially Hungarian and Romanian – all at reasonable prices.*

Wright Wine Co

The Old Smithy, Raikes Road, Skipton, North Yorkshire BD23 1NP (01756) 700886 (01756) 794175 fax (01756) 798580 e-mail sales@wineandwhisky.co.uk website www.wineandwhisky.co.uk hours Mon–Fri 9–6; Sat 10–5:30; open Sundays in December 10.30–4 cards Maestro, MasterCard, Visa discounts 10% unsplit case, 5% mixed case delivery Free within 30 miles, elsewhere at cost. G

☼ *Equally good in both Old World and New World, with plenty of good stuff at keen prices. Wide choice of half bottles.*

Peter Wylie Fine Wines

Plymtree Manor, Plymtree, Cullompton, Devon EX15 2LE (01884) 277555 fax (01884) 277557 e-mail peter@wylie-fine-wines. demon.co.uk website www.wyliefinewines.co.uk hours Mon–Fri 9–6 cards None discounts Only on unsplit cases delivery Up to 3 cases in London £20, 4 or more cases at cost. C M

☼ *Fascinating list of very old wines; Bordeaux from throughout the 20th century including Château Yquem 1847, vintage ports going back to 1904 and vintage Madeira to 1902.*

Yapp Brothers

The Old Brewery, Water Street, Mere, Wilts BA12 6DY (01747) 860423 fax (01747) 860929 e-mail sales@yapp.co.uk website www.yapp.co.uk hours Mon–Sat 9–6 cards Maestro, MasterCard, Visa discounts £6 per case on collection delivery £6 one case, 2 or more cases free. C G M T

☼ *Rhône and Loire specialists. They also have some of the hard-to-find wines of Provence, Savoie, South-West France and Corsica.*

Noel Young Wines

56 High Street, Trumpington, Cambridge CB2 9LS (01223) 566744 fax (01223) 844736 e-mail admin@nywines.co.uk website www.nywines.co.uk hours Mon–Fri 10–8, Sat 10–7, Sun 12–2 cards AmEx, Maestro, MasterCard, Visa discounts 5% for orders over £500 delivery Free over 12 bottles unless discounted en primeur Australia, Burgundy, Italy, Rhône. G M T

☼ *Fantastic wines from just about everywhere. Australia is a particular passion and there is a great Austrian list, some terrific Germans, plus beautiful Burgundies, Italians and dessert wines.*

Who's where

COUNTRYWIDE/ MAIL ORDER ONLY
Adnams
Aldi
ASDA
L'Assemblage
H & H Bancroft Wines
Bibendum Wine
Bordeaux Index
Anthony Byrne
ChateauOnline
Co-op
Devigne Wines
Nick Dobson Wines
Domaine Direct
Fine Wines of New
    Zealand
Roger Harris Wines
Jeroboams
Justerini & Brooks
Laithwaites
Lay & Wheeler
Laytons
Liberty Wines
O W Loeb
Majestic
Marks & Spencer
Millésima
Montrachet
Morrisons
Oddbins
OZ WINES
Real Wine Co
Howard Ripley
Sainsbury's
Somerfield
Stone, Vine & Sun
Sunday Times Wine Club
Tesco
Thresher
Vin du Van
Vintage Roots
Virgin Wines
Waitrose
Wine Rack
The Wine Society
Wine Treasury
Wines of Westhorpe
Peter Wylie Fine Wines
Yapp Brothers
Noel Young Wines

LONDON
Armit
Balls Brothers
Berkmann Wine Cellars
Berry Bros. & Rudd
Budgens
Corney & Barrow
Farr Vintners
Fortnum & Mason
Friarwood
Goedhuis & Co
Green & Blue
Handford Wines
Harvey Nichols
Haynes Hanson & Clark
Jeroboams
Lea & Sandeman
Moreno Wines
Philglas & Swiggot
Roberson
RSJ Wine Company
Selfridges
Waterloo Wine Co
Wimbledon Wine Cellar
The Winery

SOUTH-EAST AND HOME COUNTIES
A&B Vintners
Bacchus Wine
Berry Bros. & Rudd
Budgens
Butlers Wine Cellar
Cape Wine and Food
Les Caves de Pyrene
Flagship Wines
Le Fleming Wines
The Flying Corkscrew
Hedley Wright
Maison du Vin
Quaff Fine Wine
    Merchant
Turville Valley Wines

WEST AND SOUTH-WEST
Averys Wine Merchants
Bennetts Fine Wines
Berkmann Wine Cellars
Great Western Wine
Haynes Hanson & Clark
Hicks & Don
Laymont & Shaw
The Nobody Inn
Christopher Piper Wines
Reid Wines
Savage Selection
Peter Wylie Fine Wines
Yapp Brothers

EAST ANGLIA
Adnams
Budgens
Anthony Byrne
Corney & Barrow

Hicks & Don
Seckford Wines
T & W Wines
Noel Young Wines

MIDLANDS
Bat & Bottle
Connolly's
Croque-en-Bouche
deFINE
Gauntleys
Harvey Nichols
S H Jones
Nickolls & Perks
Noble Rot Wine
    Warehouses
Oxford Wine Co
Portland Wine Co
Selfridges
Stevens Garnier
Tanners

WALES
Ballantynes Wine
    Merchants
Irma Fingal-Rock
Moriarty Vintners
Terry Platt Wine
    Merchants
Tanners

NORTH
Berkmann Wine Cellars
Booths
D Byrne
Great Northern Wine
Halifax Wine Co
Harvey Nichols
Martinez Wines

Nidderdale Fine Wines
Penistone Court Wine
    Cellars
Playford Ros
Richardson & Sons
Selfridges
Frank Stainton Wines
Vinceremos
Whitesides of Clitheroe
Wright Wine Co

SCOTLAND
Berkmann Wine Cellars
Cockburns of Leith
Corney & Barrow
Friarwood
Peter Green & Co
Harvey Nichols
Linlithgow Wines
Raeburn Fine Wines
Valvona & Crolla
Villeneuve Wines

NORTHERN IRELAND
Direct Wine Shipments
James Nicholson
Winemark

CHANNEL ISLANDS
Sommelier Wine Co

FRANCE
ChateauOnline
Millésima
Oddbins
Sainsbury's
Tesco Vin Plus
Wine & Beer World